AIRCRAFT
AND
AVIATION
STAMPS

*To my four grandchildren who bring me such immense joy:
Hollie May, William Dennis, Isabella Amelie and Emily Mabel.*

TRANSPORT
PHILATELY
SERIES

AIRCRAFT
AND
AVIATION
STAMPS

HOWARD PILTZ

PEN & SWORD
TRANSPORT

AN IMPRINT OF PEN & SWORD BOOKS LTD.
YORKSHIRE – PHILADELPHIA

First published in Great Britain in 2020 by
Pen and Sword Transport
An imprint of
Pen & Sword Books Ltd
Yorkshire - Philadelphia

Copyright © Howard Piltz, 2020

ISBN 978 1 47387 186 1

The right of Howard Piltz to be identified as Author of this work has been asserted
by him in accordance with the Copyright, Designs and Patents Act 1988.

A CIP catalogue record for this book is available from the British Library.

Typeset in PT Serif 11/14 by Aura Technology and Software Services, India
Printed and bound in India by Replika Press Pvt. Ltd.

Pen & Sword Books Ltd incorporates the Imprints of Pen & Sword Books
Archaeology, Atlas, Aviation, Battleground, Discovery, Family History, History,
Maritime, Military, Naval, Politics, Railways, Select, Transport, True Crime, Fiction,
Frontline Books, Leo Cooper, Praetorian Press, Seaforth Publishing, Wharncliffe
and White Owl.

For a complete list of Pen & Sword titles please contact

PEN & SWORD BOOKS LIMITED
47 Church Street, Barnsley, South Yorkshire, S70 2AS, England
E-mail: enquiries@pen-and-sword.co.uk
Website: www.pen-and-sword.co.uk

or

PEN AND SWORD BOOKS
1950 Lawrence Rd, Havertown, PA 19083, USA
E-mail: Uspen-and-sword@casematepublishers.com
Website: www.penandswordbooks.com

CONTENTS

INTRODUCTION

TO BEGIN WITH

Early in 2018, I was wandering through my favourite internet sites looking for further stamps to add to my collection and just as I was preparing the manuscript for this book, I came across stamps from a country I'd never heard of - Niuafo´ou – where?

One of the wonders of the late twentieth century and through to today is the ability to use the Internet to research your subject, to try to find out where on earth that strangely named place really IS; as it happens it is the northern-most island of the Tonga archipelago in the southern Pacific Ocean. Read what I found out in the chapter on the Pacific Region.

THE TWO SIDES

Collecting stamps brings a wonderful new view of the world to the collector, celebrated in the more formal title of the philatelist, who is led through an amazing world of knowledge, where the inquisitive mind can ponder the mysteries of bygone times. Why, you may ask, do British postage stamps never, but *never* boast their country of origin? And of course, we've already stumbled upon Niuafo´ou.

Likewise, someone with a worldly interest in transport may find that the hobby will lead him – or her – all over the world, if not literally then as a by-product of studying the subject. There are a great many transport professionals who have worked on several different continents throughout their working lives to bring the benefit of their skills to areas one might consider under-developed in the areas of public transport. Personally, I have spent many years as an enthusiast of most forms of public transport and have been to places that until the advent of cheap air travel seemed quite outlandish. I have been to a lake on Vancouver Island on Canada's Pacific coast where lived the world's two largest flying boats regaling in the name of 'Mars', whilst it seemed to me at the time – I was 14 – quite exciting, but utterly easy in 1959, to talk myself onto the inaugural KLM Viscount flight from Manchester to Amsterdam only to find there was no return flight home that day, memories of the heart-clutching scream from Dad over the phone will never fade: 'You're *WHERE*?'. Then there was another flight, not much later but this time with permission – and paid for – to go plane-spotting alone to the Paris Air Show. Not many years later, I visited the USA to look for the last gasps of two iconic forms of American transport – PCC trams in Newark, NJ, and the Pennsylvania Railroad GG1 electric locomotives. I could also go on a little too long about getting rather merry drinking the local brews in places like Prague, Lisbon or the countryside around Brussels whilst chasing trams.

Coming Together with Works of Art

At first sight it might seem a little odd that one should wish to combine these two totally disparate hobbies, but by good fortune I happen to have a liking for both subjects and a long time ago began to appreciate that in stamps one could find the wonderful combination of transport history told within a glorious gallery of miniature works of art. Watch through the ages as the reproduction techniques on stamps have developed from simple monochrome etchings with carefully sculpted framework such as this 1924 stamp from Bolivia.

To the untutored eye the detail is not readily apparent and some time must be spent on the country's language and its currency to fully appreciate this little gem. Interestingly, apart from a very few definitives of the 1890s and 1900s it was to be 1963 before a British stamp would appear with more than one colour; not even the UK's 1953 Coronation stamps boasted more. The accepted appearance developed first to two or three colours and then, as with everything else towards the end of the twentieth century, convention went out of the window as we saw full colour art-work and the use of photographs – and quite often in these days of digital photography – fairly heavily manipulated ones at that.

What's in this collection?

There will be several different formats that the reader will find mentioned in this book, and there follows a brief summary for the novice philatelist:

Mint stamps: unused stamps, un-marked on their face and with the gum on the back still intact. It used to be the habit of collectors to stick gummed, paper hinges to the back of their stamps for mounting in an album. The damage that this does for serious collectors has discredited this practice and one will often find these days the initials MNH (Mint, not hinged) within the description of a particular stamp or set of stamps.

Used stamps: As the terminology states, postage stamps that have been used for the purpose for which they were designed, indicating that the due fee for the service required has been paid, and stuck on the envelope or parcel as proof. Hence they bear a post-mark (sometimes referred to as a 'franking' or 'cancellation') to indicate the office of cancellation and will undoubtedly have no gum on the back but traces of the paper they had been stuck to. Apart from its rarity value, a collector will look for how heavy the post-mark appears on the stamp and how well the backing has been removed, a thinning of the stamp itself or loss of any part of the face or the perforations will render the stamp valueless, scrap, or – where it is a particularly rare example – seriously devalued.

Definitives: What one could describe as the regular, run-of-the-mill stamps that one would get on a day-to-day basis.

Miniature Sheets, or mini-sheets are often produced by the issuing postal authority using either one stamp with a border that might be an extension of the illustration on the stamp, or several stamps within that border, surrounded by a description.

Here is a very nice example issued by Gibraltar and showing seaplanes and flying boats from the improbable – a 1911 'le Canard' built by Frere Voisin – to the oh-so-nearly in the case of the Saunders Roe Princess that showed such huge promise but eventually succumbed to the vagaries of politics.

Presentation packs: Here we have one of the philatelist's best friends for not only is there usually one, pristine and mint example of each stamp in any particular issue but they are presented behind a clear film hinged so that the stamps may be withdrawn if one wishes, and then within a card wallet often containing sometimes quite copious details of the event celebrated as well as technical information, and then all within a cellophane envelope for virtually indefinite preservation. Shown here is a pack issued on the Isle of Man in 2016 to mark the 150th anniversary of the Royal Aeronautical Society together with eight stamps inside that mark some of the outstanding events in aeronautical history.

First Day Cover (FDC): If the Presentation Pack is not your thing then join the many collectors of the FDC, as its name implies, posted and franked on the first day the stamps go into circulation and so gaining a certain cachet. The envelope, often referred to as a cover, may be a product of the issuing post office and cancelled with a special, carefully-applied franking, but that is by no means certain and quite often you may find that a

specialist dealer or the organisation involved may have produced their own cover, obtained the stamps in advance and even having a hand in designing the special franking. The cover shown comes from Gibraltar again with a novel approach showing 'Wings of Prey' of two totally different genres.

Specialist Covers: These are covers that are not designed for use on the first day of issue of a particular stamp or set of stamps. An organisation, maybe with an eye on the commercial opportunity, will produce a specially printed envelope to commemorate an event even if no special stamps have been issued, use a postage stamp that may or may not be of particular relevance, and possibly apply a special franking. Often very attractive and collectable, but of value only within a small circle of collectors.

PHQ Cards: 'PHQ' stands for Postal Headquarters but here refers to reproduction of stamps on postcards; all items published by the British Post Office are given a number that is prefixed by the letters PHQ. The first card issued was the 3p W.G. Grace stamp from the set commemorating County Cricket; issued on 16 May 1973, this card was numbered PHQ 1 and the numbering sequence has continued to the present day. There are several sets that replicate stamps illustrating our hobby.

What is *not* generally in my collection are stamps produced where there is quite obviously no intention to satisfy a need to provide a postal service in the issuing country.

So, dear reader, follow me now on a rather circuitous tour of our world with the aid of the various artists involved and my fascination with transport through the medium of the postage stamp.

THE WORLD OF AVIATION THROUGH THE MEDIUM OF POSTAGE STAMPS

For the third book in this series on public transport issues featured on postage stamps, once again I will combine two of my life-long hobbies and look at stamps that feature the huge subject of aviation, whether it be a brief venture into aviation history or, as is often the case, the celebration of a country's prowess in manufacturing or operation.

Aviation was an early subject for stamps as often issuing authorities would produce special ones for air-mail services. The stamp illustrated here and issued in 1935 doesn't show the earliest aircraft used but nevertheless shows us graphically the pioneering days of carrying the post by air. In the days when the latest Boeing 747 freighter can carry almost 140 tons of freight, the weight of the average letter can be considered almost insignificant but in those early days and until well after the Second World War, great care needed to be taken in considering the medium that we used. Special lightweight papers were available in pads together with  envelopes, whilst the British Post Office would sell you a sheet of lightweight blue paper with a stamp of suitable value already printed on it together with guides to show the user how to fold it up (rather like origami) into an envelope size for posting and inevitably bearing a little blue 'Air Mail' sticker top-left that is an anachronistic left-over into the twenty-first century, for surely these days ALL overseas mail goes by air unless surface mail is specifically requested.

I do not try to produce an exhaustive survey encompassing every country and every issue; for that one needs to refer to major catalogues issues by such well-known authorities as Stanley Gibbons Plc. in the UK and its contemporaries in other parts of the world. Rather, I have woven history and anecdotes around items in my own extensive collection, and often look in my albums to try to understand why sometimes a particular country will be represented by bulging sections whilst others may be represented by but one or two stamps. So follow the story around the world in roughly an eastern journey starting naturally in my own home of the United Kingdom, learning about some of the national histories on the way and admiring the work of some extremely accomplished artists that mean philatelists and lovers of flight together can enjoy many beautiful miniature works of art.

THE BRITISH ISLES

lthough it was on 9 September 1911 that Britain's first official aerial post was inaugurated between Hendon and Windsor of all places, it wasn't until 1963 that the Royal Mail issued its first stamps bearing the image of an aircraft, in that case a rather crude one of a helicopter. Gradually we began to see more and more, and surely unique is such a fascinating history told by one humble stamp of 1967 shows an Armstrong Whitworth Argosy freighter in the colours of British European Airways, the State-owned airline tasked with serving internal and European destinations and that was eventually merged with BOAC (q.v.) to form the British Airways of today.

The Argosy was designed to fill a perceived need for a pure freighter on short to medium distances. Its first flight was in 1959 and leant heavily on the success of the Vickers

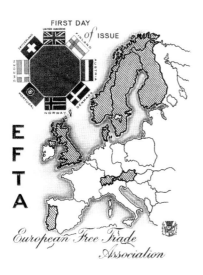

Viscount (another aircraft of the post-war era designed for short to medium distance flights, but as a passenger carrier). Both used Rolls Royce Dart turbo-prop engines and whilst the Viscount sold in substantial numbers world-wide, the Argosy only sold in small numbers to BEA and the RAF, as well as the USA as the economics of a specialised freighter at the time proved its downfall and all were out of service in a very short period of time.

Interestingly, this stamp also bears the initials EFTA – the European Free Trade Area that was established by the Stockholm Convention in 1960 as an alternative trading block to the European Economic Community that later became the European Union. Great Britain was a part of that body but later switched sides. EFTA still operates and its members are Iceland, Liechtenstein, Norway, and Switzerland.

To the lovers of commercial aviation there is always a favourite, either aesthetically or technically. In Britain, few will disagree that the Vickers VC-10 and its longer sibling the Super VC-10 holds top-spot, whilst in the United States anyone who argues against the true elegance of the Lockheed Constellation is risking universal opprobrium. In the world at large, though, whether one looks at the professional or enthusiast fraternity there is just one flying machine that transcends all others for both beauty and achievement and that is Concorde, a product of the jet age, of man's desperate endeavour to continually improve his lot and it was the work of a combined effort of British and French engineers (and no little of politicians) that produced undoubtedly the world's most elegant aircraft. This is acknowledged if one looks at how Concorde is addressed: not 'a Concorde' or 'this' or 'that' Concorde but just, simply 'Concorde' as if she was a member of our family, or the one aircraft in the travellers' fraternity that was special. I never flew in Concorde, but I am proud to say I know someone who did!

To illustrate Concorde by the medium of the postage stamp is not quite as easy as you would have hoped, for whilst the postal authorities of both Britain and France produced issues to celebrate the first flight, understandably neither agency quite managed to pull-off the grace of her in flight. Anybody who saw the first flight on television that has so often been repeated will no-doubt recall the words "She flies!, Concorde flies at last!" uttered by an ecstatic Raymond Baxter, one of the BBC's early commentators. Chosen to mark Concorde's place in history is a presentation pack issued in 2002, with a set of five stamps to mark the 50th anniversary of passenger jet aviation, and the stamp captures the ogival plan-form of the wing shape in a most dramatic way.

Both the previous set and this illustration shows details of the afore-mentioned Vickers VC10, not only showing us the sheer elegance of this 1960s-era airliner but also the esteem in which the type was held in the British aviation world. That its commercial success was eclipsed by the Boeing 707 and its contemporaries from the US had as much to do with the better operating economics of the latter as it did to the meddling of the British government and its puppet flag carrier British Overseas Airlines Corporation (BOAC). What we see here is the Air Mail Letter, sometimes referred to as the aerogramme, usually deceptively large and that one followed the fold-lines to leave the envelope-shaped item we see here. Every post office had brass, classical scales to weigh your letter very carefully. Britain's Royal Mail issued these air mail letters until the mid-1980s but if you take something to the Post Office in the UK today for sending abroad the attendant will automatically plonk on your letter a little blue 'Air Mail, Par Avion' sticker, most surely the last vestiges of air-mail stamps or stationery in the UK.

Post & Go stamps are variable rate postage stamps printed on self-adhesive labels and sold from stamp vending machines by Royal Mail in the United Kingdom. The first trials were carried out in 2004 and by 2008 over 700 machines were rolled out across the country. Not all those sold were illustrated as these are and a definitive example is also shown.

Jersey Post, Guernsey Post, and the Royal Gibraltar Post Office have also followed the Royal Mail.

Before leaving the products of the Royal Mail it is nice to visit one of the more light-hearted aspects of our hobby where a cover is produced for a special event, here the air-show at Hendon, London in 1981 featuring the late Wing-Commander Ken H. Wallis MBE RAF (Ret'd), (1916-2013) who signed several of the covers. He took an earlier American Benson design and produced the enigmatic autogyro that bears his name and will forever be associated with the James Bond film *You Only Live Twice*, where a WA-116 machine named *Little Nellie* was seen, supposedly flown by Bond and fitted with rockets!

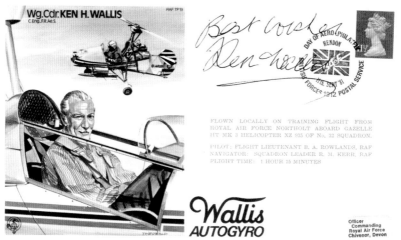

The Channel Islands

Set in the English Channel nearer to France than the UK, these islands are an archipelago consisting of two Crown dependencies: the Bailiwick of Jersey, which is the largest of the islands; and the Bailiwick of Guernsey, consisting of Guernsey, Alderney, Sark and some smaller islands. They are considered the remnants of the Duchy of Normandy and, although they are not part of the United Kingdom, that country is responsible for the defence and international relations of the islands.

The first aeroplane to land on Jersey did so on the beach at West Park, on the Island's south coast, in August 1912. However, it was to be another twenty-five years before the new Jersey Airport was officially opened on 10 March 1937 and celebrated here by one of an extensive series issued by the Jersey Post sixty years later and showing many of the types that have operated from the island in that time. It is particularly happy to report that during the writing of this book, the De Havilland Heron 2 shown – G-AORG – has returned to Jersey for onward preservation.

Coming right up to date, in 2017 Jersey Post issued several stamps to commemorate the end of the First World War – or as it was known then the Great War – and in line

with my own opinion that Jersey's stamps are some of the best, here we see some splendid artwork illustrating the various aircraft that took part in that conflict.

Guernsey, or more correctly the Bailiwick of Guernsey, was separated from the Dukedom and Duchy of Normandy under the terms of the Treaty of Le Goulet in 1204. The islands have always valued their links to the outside world and have produced several issues relating to aviation. During the Second World War, when the Channel Islands became the only part of the British Isles to be invaded by the Germans, UK stamps became difficult to obtain and these are the island's first postage stamps, issued in 1941.

In 1969 Guernsey Post was created and since then Guernsey postage stamps have been issued on a regular basis, whilst from 1983, Guernsey began issuing specific stamps designated Alderney for use in that island.

This 1989 set was issued to mark two subjects, the 50th anniversary of Guernsey's airport and of the island's association with the RAF's 201 Squadron. Interestingly, at least one example of each aircraft illustrated survives either operational or in a museum except the de Havilland DH.86 Express, a four-engined development of their long-running series of passenger bi-planes that culminated in the well-known DH.89 Dragon Rapide (also shown here) and DH.90 Dragonfly. A further dedicated series of

stamps to mark the 201 (Guernsey's Own) Squadron was issued in 2018.

The Alderney set is quite unusual in that it concentrates on but one airline native to Guernsey – Aurigny Air Services, the name being old-Norman for Alderney. The airline was

formed in 1968 to serve as an intra-island carrier together with connections to both the British and French mainland but came under the direct control of the States of Guernsey in 2003, and this set issued in 2008 marks its fortieth birthday and as such the oldest established airline in the UK after Loganair.

Aurigny became well known for its operation of a large fleet of Britten Norman Trilanders built not-far away on another island, Isle of Wight, first flying in 1970 and one in particular developed an almost cult following – G-JOEY, illustrated on the 40p stamp and which was preserved upon its retirement in 2015.

Eire

The Republic of Ireland comes under the all-embracing category of the British Isles and a worth-while First Day cover shown here neatly encompasses 75 years of the Country's national airline Aer Lingus (the Irish *aerloingeas* meaning 'air fleet') that started operation in 1936 and shows us the airline's first aircraft – the DH Dragon EI-ABI – in stark contrast to the huge Boeing 747 of today. Another Dragon bears the same registration and is still flown occasionally by the airline as a salute to its history.

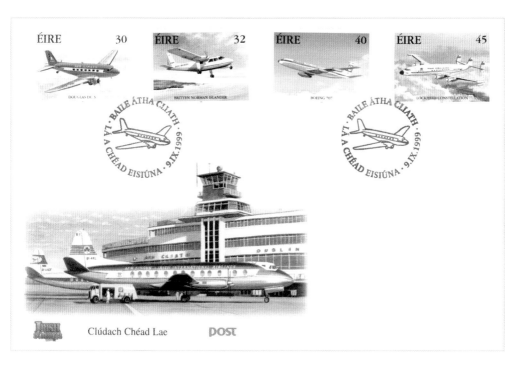

ÉIRE 30 ÉIRE 32 ÉIRE 40 ÉIRE 45

DOUGLAS DC 3   BRITTEN NORMAN ISLANDER   BOEING "707"   LOCKHEED CONSTELLATION

Clúdach Chéad Lae   POST

Ireland was never a rich country until well into the second half of the twentieth century, with little private aviation and an embryonic national airline. Even in the early twenty-first century with ownership of the airline passing to IAG, the holding company of British Airways and other European airlines, the predominant livery of Aer Lingus remains vivid green as is illustrated in this next FDC by the Dakota and Viscount we see here.

Irish International Airline was established separately to operate flights westwards to North America providing a connection with the huge migrant Irish population in that part of the world. The operator initially used Lockheed Constellations followed by Boeing 720s and 707s and as it was fully merged with Aer Lingus, progressed to Airbus A330s, a type still used today. Finally, there is a very attractive view of a Trans World Airlines Lockheed Super Constellation that visited Ireland for many years after the Second World War, catering for the same market in the New World.

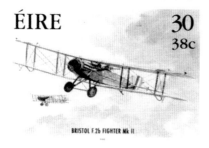

The Republic of Ireland has long had a small military air operation known as the Irish Air Corps, established in 1924, the air component of the Defence Forces of Ireland. Through a fleet of fixed and rotary wing aircraft, it provides military support to the Army and Naval Service, together with non-military services such as Garda air support, air ambulance, fisheries protection and the Ministerial Air Transport Service. The primary airbase is Casement Aerodrome located at Baldonnel, County Dublin. This strip of self-adhesive stamps issued in 2000 illustrates some of the many types used over the years and is also noteworthy for showing the change-over at that time from the Irish punt to the Euro.

EUROPE

Portugal

Starting with the western-most country, Portugal has a great history of adventurers and colonisation starting in the fifteenth century to include Brazil, briefly parts

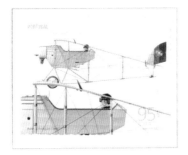 

Portugal
Famous Aircraft of the Twentieth Century

of North America, various territories in Africa and even Macau in the Far East, and it was the latter's passing back to China in 1999 that saw the final chapter written in this part of Portugal's history. Today the country is known for its wines as well as sandy beaches of the Algarve

Aviation came too late to have any major part in the countries expansionist excursions but of course is a major player today in the tourist industry.

The stamps chosen are a particularly attractive set issued in 1999 to mark 75 years of military aviation. Of interest is the inclusion of two currencies as introduction of the Euro had just taken the place of the national Escudo.

Spain; surrounding Portugal on two sides of the Iberian Peninsula, Spain is much larger, a country of over

46 million people according to a 2016 poll and today known as a popular holiday destination that represents the country's largest source of revenue. The earliest stamps featuring aviation were very early – 1926 – and were for air-mail letters, either connecting the capital Madrid with Manila in the Philippines or crossing the Atlantic, both precarious journeys in those days.

Coming forward to 1955, Corres – the Spanish postal authority – issued another set of stamps for use on air-mail letters, but all eleven featured the same, elegant engraving of a Lockheed L1049 Super Constellation, differing only in colour and value.

In 1961, Corres issued a set of five stamps to celebrate the 50th Anniversary of Spanish aviation.

Naturally, the first two stamps feature the work of the Spanish, the 1pta (peseta) stamp illustrates a Cierva C.30A autogyro which although British-built was the design of Spanish engineer and pilot Juan de la Cierva. Then there

is the 2pta stamp that shows a CASA-built Junkers Do-J Wal flying boat. Construcciones Aeronáuticas S.A. (CASA) was a Spanish aircraft manufacturer which was founded in 1923 and began manufacturing aircraft the following year.

In 1999, it became a subsidiary of the EADS (European Aeronautic Defence and Space Company) better known as builders of the Airbus range of airliners.

Finally, like a great many nations and airlines, the Spanish carrier Iberia operated the iconic Boeing 747 'Jumbo Jet' with great pride and in an attempt to stay competitive. Here we see one such aircraft flying over Madrid in a stamp issued in 1971 to mark the 50th Anniversary of the Spanish air-mail service.

Gibraltar stands at a strategic position at the entrance to the Mediterranean and is a British Overseas Territory on Spain's south coast. It is dominated by the Rock of Gibraltar, a 426m-high limestone ridge and, as such is much valued by British military strategists. Unavoidably, the Rock has a major presence on almost all stamps issued there. This particular Presentation Pack is one of three issued in 1982 to hold the new definitive stamps which ran to fifteen stamps with face-values from 1p to £5 and in view of its heritage, these stamps are dominated by aircraft of British manufacture or operation.

Almost forgotten today are post-war types such as the Vickers Viking on the 2p stamp, designed using many structures from the wartime Wellington bomber as a Douglas Dakota replacement shown in the 1p stamp but now long since vanished; the Airspeed Ambassador (or Elizabethan as it was known by BEA, the only airline to buy it from the manufacturers) was rapidly eclipsed by the first turboprop airlines the Vickers Viscount; and on the 10p stamp the Vickers Vanguard which was a development of the Viscount but sold in far fewer numbers and has again long since retired from our skies.

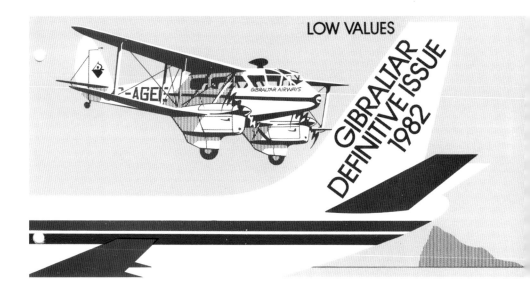

France holds a very special place in the annals of aviation history. With the possible exception of the USA, no other country can demand so many entries in this book with its profusion of firsts, eminent aviators and builders from Blériot, right through to today's Airbus Industries, a pan-European business based in Toulouse.

We must start way back in 1782 when the Montgolfier brothers first built a balloon at their paper factory that lifted itself using hot air and with the active encouragement of Louis XVI succeeded in building a bigger balloon that was able to carry two men the following year, a true first and illustrated here is a First Day Cover with stamp marking the 200th anniversary of that great event.

Interestingly, national policy ever since has been to encourage aviation in all forms and today a visit to a small aerodrome like Toussus-le-Noble, some 25kms (15 miles) south-west from Paris will overwhelm anyone used to the sleepy aerodromes of the UK.

Undoubtedly one of France's most celebrated aviators was Louis Blériot (1872-1936), an aviator, inventor and engineer who in 1909 became world famous for making the first aeroplane flight across the English Channel and in so doing winning the prize of £1,000 offered by the *Daily Mail* newspaper. The stamp shown here, whilst not the first to feature Blériot, was issued in 2009 to celebrate

the centenary of that achievement and clearly shows the man and his machine.

French aircraft manufacturers were almost as prolific as those celebrated, contemporary airmen and women and this 1954 set shows us some of the larger concerns and their wares.

A lovely set from 1984 gives some idea of the vast array of products in the inter-war years.

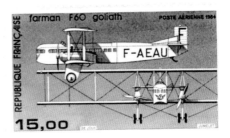

But wait a minute. Look at this stamp 2 Franc stamp below – same as one of those in the previous set but with a different value!

Confused? France's national currency until the arrival of the Euro at the turn of the century was the franc but inflation meant that prices were being quoted in hundreds of francs if not thousands and beyond for high value items – just see that 1954 set – so the franc was devalued in 1960 by a value of one hundred and the new, more manageable currency was officially known as the nouveau franc, or nf, although within a few years the nouveau bit was dropped as everyone got used to the new currency.

No review of French aviation would be complete with the mention of three

iconic products, the first being the Sud-Aviation SE.210 Caravelle noted as the first short/medium-range jet airliner and also the first to position its engines at the rear for a relatively quiet cabin and clean wings for maximum efficiency. Its maiden flight was in 1955 and the 282 built operated in every continent included the United States where United Airlines' order spurred every other major builder to develop their own clone.

Together with the UK, France was instrumental in developing one of the world's greatest technical achievements – Concorde – and not to celebrate that on a stamp would be unforgiveable and here she is grouped with four other very noteworthy examples of French innovative design – I can attest to the exceptional design of the Citroen 2cv car having owned several.

Germany is a nation of immensely proud people. Its history has been an ever-changing one, born out of several smaller countries in the nineteenth century, been at the centre of two global conflicts; part of it subsumed by a fundamentalist but flawed ideology and finally today stands high in both the European Union and also one of the world's greatest aeroplane makers – Airbus Industry.

As a result, German stamps bear several names of origin and here we see three stamps issued

in 1956 by what was generally known as East Germany, to mark the establishment of a post-war airline Deutsche Lufthansa (literally German Airline). Having become part of the Soviet Bloc, the East German operation naturally looked east for their fleet and the Ilyushin IL-14 was a contemporary of the American Convair 240, Douglas DC-4/6 and the British Vickers Viking. The IL-14 first flew in 1950 and although never common outside eastern Europe, total production amounted to 1,348 examples, the last one not retired by the Russian CAA until 2005!

What marked postage stamps out as valuable and attractive sources of material for the public was the various series of stamps like these that in twenty-four values covered a huge spectrum of aviation history from the Montgolfier balloon to the Boeing 747 'Jumbo Jet' and issued in West Germany by the Deutsche Bundespost in several batches between 1978-80 and included a similar series for the isolated West Berlin which at the time was still an enclave within East Germany. All the

SIKORSKY S-55 1949

FOKKER F 27 FRIENDSHIP 1955

VICKERS VISCOUNT 1950

SUD AVIATION CARAVELLE 1955

HEINKEL HE 70 1932

DORNIER WAL 1922

JUNKERS W 33 BREMEN 1928

FOCKE-WULF FW 61 1936

stamps include 50 per cent addition as a charitable donation and marked 'Fur Die Jugend' or 'Youth Welfare' in the right hand margin. Another of the set is shown here mounted on a PHQ card issued by the postal authority and showing the elegant lines of the Lockheed Super Constellation L-1049G in the colours of Lufthansa.

Issued in 1972 is this pair of stamps that illustrate some aviation activities in Eastern Germany certainly at the miniscule end of subjects on stamps.

The 5pf (pfennig) stamp illustrates the Kamov Ka-26 helicopter from Romania and given the NATO code-name 'hoodlum', a light utility machine small enough to land on the back of a truck which uses a coaxial main rotor configuration obviating the need for a tail rotor.

The 10pf stamp shows the LET Z-37 Čmelák – Bumblebee – an agricultural aircraft made in what was then Czechoslovakia

The two sides of Germany in the post-war era came together in 1990 in a very public fashion and in the full glare of the world's television when first the Berlin Wall and other unnatural borders dissolved to the delight of everyone. Postage stamps also came under a unified Deutche Bundespost and very quickly took on the simple title Deutschland and the set shown here from 2008 illustrate a wide cross-section of some very characteristic German production.

Scandinavia is a region in Northern Europe with strong historical, cultural, and linguistic ties. Denmark lies to the north of Germany whilst separated by the Øresund Sound is Norway and Sweden sitting next to each other further north and included in the term 'Nordic countries' that includes Finland, Iceland, and their associated territories (Greenland, the Faroe Islands and the Åland Islands).

Denmark. This country's commercial airline industry started with Det Danske Luftfartselskab A/S that traded as

Danish Airlines, established in the closing months of the First World War 1. This was subsumed into Scandinavian Airlines System together with Swedish and Norwegian contemporaries in 1946 initially to pool trans-Atlantic services and in 1951 to integrate all commercial operations.

This card above was produced to commemorate the introduction into service of the elegant Douglas DC-7C airliner that inaugurated over-the-pole services from Europe to the Far East. This airliner was the final Douglas airliner to use piston engines, ending a long line of DC models going back to the DC-1 of 1933 and about to be eclipsed by jets starting in the late fifties.

The lovely presentation pack, overleaf, from 2006 clearly shows its value, telling us that the country had its own aviation industry from 1937 when Skandinavisk Aero Industri was established and built around 200 aircraft until 1954 and all termed KZ after its founders Kramme and Zeuthen. It was issued to mark the centenary of one of the country's early aviation pioneers and inventors Jacob Christian Ellehammer, although other sources give his birth as 1907. The other stamps show a military trainer, the KZ.IV, a communications and ambulance aircraft and finally from 1947 the KZ.VII, a club trainer, examples of which are believed to be still flying in Finland and Switzerland.

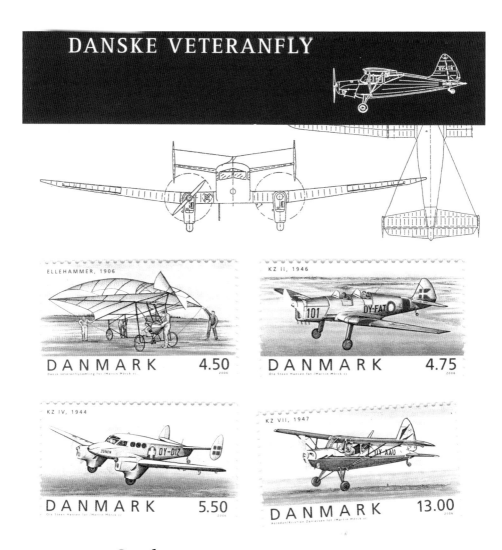

Sweden retains an important member of the global aerospace and defence industry with Saab AB, founded in 1937 today employing over 16,000 people worldwide but their prowess has never been celebrated seriously on the country's stamps. However, this attractive miniature sheet was issued in 1984 illustrating some of the country's aviation and does show the Scandia 24-32 seat airliner, development of which was started in 1944 and entered service in 1950.

Only eighteen were built, serving airlines in Scandinavia and South America so could hardly be considered a success.

Iceland is a Nordic island country in the North Atlantic covering an area of just over 100,000sq.km, with a population of approximately 350,000 and is the most sparsely populated country in Europe. The capital and largest city is Reykjavík which is home to over two-thirds of the population. Iceland is volcanically and geologically active.

Being in the middle of the Atlantic Ocean and bordered by the Arctic Circle, aviation has taken on a character less familiar to continental Europe and these colourful stamps issued between 1993 and 2009 illustrate aviation's nautical nature.

One interesting aspect of Iceland's aviation is the country's position between Europe and the USA. Founded in 1937, Flugfélag Íslands ehf. is now part of the Icelandair Group quoted on the NASDAQ Stock exchange in the US but based at the island's principal airport Keflavik near Reykjavik. Not being part of any global national agreements on fares, airlines based on the island have competed aggressively with the added advantage that in early post-war years, when other carriers were struggling to cross the Atlantic non-stop, the natural hub of Iceland made life a lot easier and even today some great deals can be found. Whilst the Dakota and Fokker aircraft we see here would not have been used for such services, the Boeing 757 definitely does and a look at arrivals and departures at Keflavik shows a huge number of European and North American destinations.

Poland is one of many eastern European countries that used to belong to the Soviet Bloc, under Communist rule and ideology. Until the fall of the Soviet era in late 1991 and the country joining the European Union in 2004, things tended to be very backward outside the major cities and I can attest to the significant use of the horse and cart until then. Today of course, things are a little different and the country thrives.

The country has long had an indigenous aviation industry, concentrating on the smaller end of the spectrum and the set of six stamps shown here were issued in 1978 celebrating the 50th anniversary of the Polish Aero Club and illustrate some of Poland's light aircraft from the earliest flying machines to more recent craft such as the motorised glider as well as some of the luminaries of the day.

Poland's national airline is LOT Polish Airlines, formally known as Polskie Linie Lotnicze LOT S.A. ('lot' being the Polish for 'flight') and the nation's flag carrier. Based in

Warsaw and established on 29 December 1928, it is one of the world's oldest airlines still in operation with a fleet of over 70 aircraft and is state owned. Although today the fleet is predominantly of Western manufacture, in the Soviet era they came from within and here we see a 1979 stamp celebrating LOT's 50th Anniversary and shows an early Dutch Fokker F.VIIb/3m and what was in the Seventies the pride of the airline – an Ilyushin IL-62M trans-continental airliner that bore a strong resemblance to the British Vickers VC-10, whilst from 2004 we have a FDC celebrating 75 years of the airlines history and culminating with an image of the Boeing 767.

The Czech Republic. Until 1993, Czechoslovakia had been another country emerging from the collapsed Soviet bloc but an amicable spilt that year saw The Czech Republic and Slovakia go their separate ways. Today, the former has considered a change yet again to Czechia but this move has not been popular and thought in many circles to be too close a name to Chechnya, an unhappy province of Russia. To outsiders, the country is famed for its ornate castles and native beers; the capital is Prague (Praha) and is home to wonderful architecture that escaped depredation of the two world wars, to a grand ninth-century Prague Castle, a preserved medieval old town and the statue-lined Charles Bridge.

This single stamp from 1967 beautifully illustrates the charms of the city together with an illustration of a Tupolev Tu-134 airliner to qualify it for inclusion in this work.

A rather delightful set of stamps also issued in 1967 illustrates some of the indigenous products of the country's small aviation industry well known for its output at the smaller end including agricultural types and gliders

The Czech airline is CSA, (České aerolinie, a.s.) which was formed in 1923 and came under the control of the Soviets in 1948; thus its fleet was dominated by Soviet type for some years and was the first foreign carrier to order Tupolev jets at the very start of the jet age and became the world's third jet operator in 1957, flying Tu-104A twin engined jets and this set from 1973 marking the airline's 50th anniversary illustrate the principle types of that era.

Emerging from Eastern domination, the airline struggles against established western operators and the loss of business to fellow Soviet Bloc countries and although still operating as a separate entity has now come under the majority ownership of the charter operator Travel Service.

Ukraine. Since its emergence from the Soviet bloc in 1990 this country has had a troubled history with its dominant neighbour Russia but with a population in 2017 of in excess of 42 million people and the largest land-mass entirely within Europe, the country continues to establish itself and cement ties all over the world. One asset from the Soviet era that found itself in Ukraine was the Antonov State Company, tasked by its previous masters to build very large aircraft for the Soviet military forces and today well known for the An-22, an enormous 4 turbo-prop engined freighter, monster An-124 jet powered freighter and the yet bigger still An-225 Mriya (dream) a sole example of

which was built to carry the Buran, the Soviet version of the American Space Shuttle. Its sheer size and SIX turbo-fan jets makes it by a significant margin the world's largest aeroplane and creates a major stir (and headache for airfield operators) on its occasional visit to overseas airport.

This block of four stamps was issued in 1996 celebrating the 90th anniversary of the birth of Oleg Antonov and apart from showing the two jet freighters we also find what must be their alter-ego – the An-2, a single-engined bi-plane of 1946, mass-produced as the ideal Soviet agricultural and utility aircraft capable of putting down almost anywhere thanks to its remarkable slow speed. I recall a stroll along the cliffs of Folkestone during an air-display when a head-wind made a Hungarian-registered An-2 appear flying slower than my leisurely progress!

The Soviet Union and Russia. Today, many people confuse the two names of this title referring to one or the other with gay abandon. The Russian Federation can trace its origins back as far as the third century AD as various groupings in the region began to coalesce whilst the modern day Soviet Union grew out the Russian Revolution of 1917 and subsumed several adjacent countries that formed the Soviet bloc until its collapse in 1991.

A great many stamps came out of the Soviet Union, a good few as examples of the nation's pride in its industrial achievements. All bore the initials CCCP as did all civil aircraft as part of their registration but these are Cyrillic letters and in the rest of the world we should read SSSR, Soyuz Sovetskikh Sotsialisticheskikh Respublik, the Latin alphabet transliteration of Союз Советских Социалистических Республик.

These first stamps were issued in 1969 to show the development of Soviet civil aircraft starting with some rather ungainly creations but ending with the very early Tu-104 and IL-62 jet airliners. Soviet leaders of the day were in the habit of arriving for summit meetings abroad

in their country's latest airliners, often never seen before. Despite reticence to go into too much detail on defence, many countries, including the Soviet Union, often illustrated military as well as civil aviation and this example shows thirty years of production of Mikoyan types, the MiG-3 of 1939 and the then current MiG-23 of 1969.

When the Soviet Union collapsed, Russia carried on in a very similar vein and in the stamp world it continued to celebrate their aircraft designers and the three mini-sheets following show the man and his machines (many other well-known designers and manufacturers have also been featured) . Issued in 2002 to mark the centenary of the birth of Nikolai Kamov, the helicopter designer, is this mini-sheet of his work.

In 2009 came a similar set featuring the work of Mikhail Mil, another helicopter designer.

In 2013 a further set featuring the work for the military of Alexei Andreyevich Tupolev (Russian: Алексе́й Андре́евич Ту́полев; 1925-2001), perhaps the most prolific name in Soviet and Russian aviation.

THE EASTERN MEDITERRANIAN

hilst a great part of this area is in Asia I feel happier treating it separately.

Malta is an archipelago of islands known for historic sites related to a succession of rulers including the Romans, Moors, Knights of St John, French and British and has numerous fortresses and megalithic temples from those eras.

Malta became a British colony in 1815, serving as a way station for ships and the headquarters for the British Mediterranean Fleet. It played an important role in the Allied war effort during the Second World War and was subsequently awarded the George Cross for its bravery in the face of an Axis siege and as a result its formal title was Malta GC until the formation of an independent Republic in 1974. Its national flag still retains the GC emblem.

Boeing 720B - AIRMALTA - 1974

Vickers Vanguard - B.E.A. - 1964

Boeing 737 - AIRMALTA - 1984

Dornier Wal - S.A.N.A - 1929

A.W. Atlanta - I.A. - 1936

Douglas DC.3 Dakota - B.O.A.C. - 1948

Vickers Viscount - ALITALIA - 1958

Likewise the series of stamps issued in 1984 proudly display the GC together with a range of aircraft from the island's past and present.

Turkey. Just like Russia, where the majority of the country is in Asia, so Turkey's claim to be in Europe is very tenuous as once across the Bosphorus Strait that splits the country's capital Istanbul in half, so the vast majority of that country is in Asia too.

The country has long enjoyed its position at the cross-roads of early trade routes known as the Silk Road from all quarters of the globe and all converging here. Today, the Turkish national airline T.H.Y. (Türk Hava Yolları) operates scheduled services to 304 destinations in Europe, Asia, Africa, and the Americas, making it the largest carrier in the world by number of passenger destinations served, and these stamps issued in 1973 gives the reader a flavour of the airline.

By contrast, in 2006 we had this delightful series produced to illustrate early aircraft of the Turkish Air Force including examples by the early French builders Deperdussin and Bleriot, all reminding me very much of the well known British comedy film *Those Magnificent Men in Their Flying Machines* (Twentieth Century-Fox, 1965).

Syria. As we move further south, Syria is another country with a proud and long history today mired in a long and sad civil war that has done nothing for its people or infrastructure including the national airline Syrian Arab Airlines and at the time of writing I am unsure if it is currently operational. Before the current conflict began, aircraft from both the West and Russia were operated and this stamp, issued in 1977 shows one of the carrier's Boeing 747SP aircraft, a foreshortened version of the early 747-100 series aircraft that were developed for 'long-thin' routes with lower passenger demand. Syrian operated these aircraft into the early part of the twenty-first century, one of the last airlines to do so.

Israel lies uncomfortably close to many Arab nations that have never been happy with the imposition of the country into its current position in 1948, and consequently

security has been a top-priority ever since. The Israeli Air Force was established almost immediately after the Declaration of Independence as an arm of the Israeli Defence Force and this set of stamps was issued in 1998 to mark the 50th anniversary of the service shows three examples of war-surplus aircraft commandeered or donated in those early days.

This slightly earlier issue from 1985 is entitled 'The Beginning of Aviation in the Holyland'.

The Beginning of Aviation
in the Holy Land

The Beginning of Aviation
in the Holy Land

The Beginning of Aviation
in the Holy Land

The Beginning of Aviation
in the Holy Land

Notice that a frequent habit of Israel Post is the embellishment of the stamp sheet margins with additional illustrations or occasionally with more information so stamps adjacent to the margins have a greater cachet and this stamp issued in 2018 marks the 70th year of civil aviation in the country when El Al (Hebrew for 'To the Skies') commenced operations.

The Jewish Sabbath runs from sunset Friday to Saturday and El Al is forbidden to operate between these times, whilst a further restriction on its finances is the continual tensions in region that severally restrict tourism.

AFRICA

The continent of Africa is unique in being crossed by both Tropics and the Equator, and a significant percentage of the north and central areas is covered by the Sahara Desert, with an area of 9.2 million square kilometres, it is comparable to the area of China or the United States.

Undoubtedly the most undeveloped continent, it has been the subject of colonial control seeking to plunder natural resources and questionable governance since the early 1900s whilst large swathes of the population have been left to starve or suffer severe deprivations. In those circumstances, it is not surprising that aviation has not figured strongly, few airlines have been established and grown to maturity whilst manufacture is virtually unknown outside South Africa.

Egypt, a country linking northeast Africa with the Middle East, dates to the time of the pharaohs, with centuries-old monuments that sit alongside the fertile Nile River Valley, Giza's colossal pyramids and Great Sphinx as well as Luxor's Karnak Temple and Valley of the Kings tombs. The capital, Cairo, is home to Ottoman landmarks like Muhammad Ali Mosque and the Egyptian Museum, a trove of antiquities.

Early aviation subjects on postage stamps in Egypt illustrate the influence of foreign interests that stamped their authority on most African states in the years of Colonial expansionisms and British aircraft therefore appear predominantly here. The history of Egypt under the British lasts from 1882, when it was occupied by British forces, until 1956 when they withdrew in accordance with the Anglo-Egyptian agreement of 1954 after the Suez Crisis. During that period long distance flying undertaken by Imperial Airways and later BOAC used Cairo as a stopping-off and refuelling point.

Illustrated here is a 1926 stamp featuring a de Havilland D.H.34 of Imperial Airways whilst moving forward to 1933 we see some of a big series of stamps marking the International Congress of Aviation held in Cairo that year and we see British aircraft – an Armstrong Whitworth Atalanta – accompanied by German types of the era – the giant Dornier Do-X and a Zeppelin Airship.

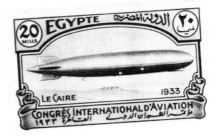

An interesting se-tenant pair shown over the page, mark the 25th anniversary of both the Egyptian Air Force and Egyptian Airlines whilst moving forward to 2007 is this startlingly different stamp marking the 75th anniversary of

the same organisations although by then the acrimony of the Suez Crisis doesn't seem to have abated and both modern aircraft now originate from the United States.

Morocco moves us along the Mediterranean Sea and to the Atlantic Ocean. Its population is principally Arab-Berber, although foreign influence, largely French and Spanish, did not have the same effect as in other African states and Morocco became independent in 1956 as Royaume du Maroc with the king at the head and having significantly greater powers than the British Monarchy.

This rather fine stamp of 1966 shows us one of five Sud Aviation Caravelles that Royal Air Maroc operated in the 1960s on all European and African routes, the choice of a French product no doubt helped by a large shareholding held by the French at that time.

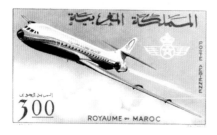

Guinee is one of those places you've heard of but can't quite place. As I said in my introduction, collecting stamps makes the brain work hard and very often considerable effort has to be made to add new files to one's personal hard disk, and here we discover the a small nation on the Atlantic coast really not far north of the Equator so generally very hot. The country's colonisation by the French in 1891 lasted until 1958 when it regained independence. Guinee's natural resources have to make the country one of Africa's richest but civil unrest, corruption and political in-fighting has meant that the population remains one of the poorest. In 2010 a new President, Alpha Conde, was elected but his efforts remain mired in controversy and the outbreak of the deadly Ebola virus killed tens of thousands in both Guinee and neighbouring counties.

As one might expect, aviation in the country is very limited but nevertheless The Office de la Poste Guineenne has issued some lovely stamps including one to mark the Olympic Games held in Tokyo in 1964 when a national Olympics Committee was established. The country has sent participants to

almost every Olympics since but has yet to win any medals.

Worthy of inclusion for no better reason than providing us with some very attractive views of well-known light aircraft is this set, issued in 1995.

I have grouped the next three countries and their stamps together as they align so strongly.

What seems so totally unacceptable today was the 1885 Berlin Conference during which colonial powers agreed the division of Africa into colonial spheres and the French took on vast areas of western Africa including **Niger, Chad** and **Gabon** principally for their natural resources. The first two of these are very large countries dominated by the Sahara Desert and are totally land-locked with a largely Islamic population and although ethnic languages now predominate, French remains the official one and this series of stamps shows the unmistakable design that was a French hallmark and would undoubtedly have been designed and printed in France, possibly even the work of the same artist, whilst very similar stamps were produced for many other French territories.

Notice that wherever possible, French aircraft predominate and the handy little not of the type shown although interestingly this single 1984 stamp from Gabon subsequent to independence in 1960 still shows the remarkable French influence embedded in the country.

Namibia straddles the Tropic of Capricorn near the southern tip of the continent and as such enjoys a generally less extreme heat than further north. Nevertheless most of its western areas are covered by the Namib desert that meets the South Atlantic Ocean in some of the world's most inhospitable coastline known to sailors, uninhabited and totally devoid of fresh water, food or shade.

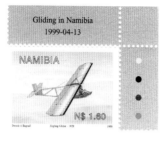

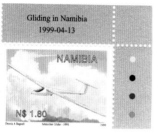

Having been colonised first by Britain, then Germany, the country was mandated back to Britain to be part of South Africa as South West Africa but it gained independence in 1990.

Noticeable in these very attractive 1999 and 2003 stamps are the vast areas of desert sands that cover so much of the continent.

South Africa, at the southern tip of the continent and bounded to the west by the South Atlantic and to the east by the Indian Ocean is distinct from the rest of the continent, known for its great wealth created by huge and valuable natural resources which have been husbanded carefully by colonial powers of the day, principally Portuguese, Dutch and British. The native populations were not treated very well culminating in the introduction of apartheid (segregation) in 1948 and not until the 1990s was this abolished, together with white rule and inspired by the redoubtable Nelson Mandela who became the first President of the Republic of South Africa (RSA) from 1994-9.

Almost universal disapproval of apartheid, especially in Africa, meant that like many aspects of the country's

economy, the development of aviation was restricted and the country has not seen many stamps on the subject but this 1993 issue is a remarkable exception.

Zimbabwe takes the traveller north and is separated from the Indian Ocean by the much larger Mozambique. It is known for its dramatic landscape and diverse wildlife, much of it within parks, reserves and safari areas. On the Zambezi River, the Victoria Falls make a thundering 108m drop into narrow Batoka Gorge.

From several organised states and kingdoms, the British South Africa Company of Cecil Rhodes first outlined the present territories during the 1890s; it became the self-governing British colony of Southern Rhodesia in 1923.

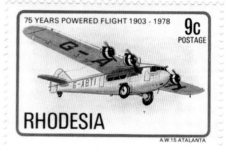

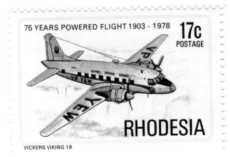

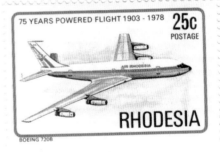

In 1965, the conservative white minority government unilaterally declared independence (the notorious UDI) as Rhodesia but democracy reigned supreme and at the time the country adopted its current name. Rhodesia issued several sets of stamps on the subject of aviation including this set issued in 1978 to mark the 75th Anniversary of Powered Flight.

I am particularly taken by the dumpy little Vickers Viking airliner that was mid-way in the genesis of post-war British aviation between the Wellington bomber and

Viscount turbo-prop and intended as a successor the venerable DC-3 'Dakota'. As such it was not sufficiently noteworthy to be considered one of the top six remarkable aircraft of those 75 years but must have been considered worthy having worked successfully in Rhodesia.

Malawi is the name adopted in 1964 when Nyasaland gained independence and after the Federation of Rhodesia and Nyasaland was dissolved the previous year. Thirty years of the London to Rhodesia air-mail service was marked in 1962 with this set of stamps nicely illustrating the progression from biplane to sea-plane and by then the ultra-modern Comet jet-liner and all three with the Monarch's icon very firmly in place.

Move forward to 1972 and Her Majesty is nowhere to be seen on the next stamps but British influence meant that the new Air Malawi used predominantly British aircraft at that time and although a government-owned enterprise, its poor financial state led to its liquidation in 2013.

Katanga proclaimed its independence from the emerging Republic of Congo when the Belgian Congo collapsed in 1960. Katanga's leaders had the support of the old colonial power Belgium and the commercial interests that mined the fledgling state's vast mineral resources. This, of course, had devastating effects to the Congolese economy and with the help of the UN and USA, the two states were reunited in early 1963.

In its short life, Katanga issued several sets of postage stamps; some of the last were these of 1961, showing two extremes of aviation at that time, a Farman

H.F.II biplane and the tail of an early Boeing 707 with a livery that betrays its origin from the Belgium national airline Sabena. These jets were still very much in their infancy showing how much the Belgians valued their former territory.

Uganda is another part of Africa that came under colonial rule, and like many countries in east Africa it was Britain which was predominant until independence in 1962. Unfortunately, much strife and a bloody guerrilla war that cost tens of thousands of lives only ceased when democracy was established in 1986.

Uganda was called the Pearl of Africa by no less an authority than Sir Winston Churchill and the country is undoubtedly one of the most stunning nations on the continent, boasting wonderful landscapes such as the snow-capped Rwenzori Mountains and the immense Lake Victoria whilst the Bwindi Impenetrable National Park is home to the famed mountain gorillas. Neighbouring

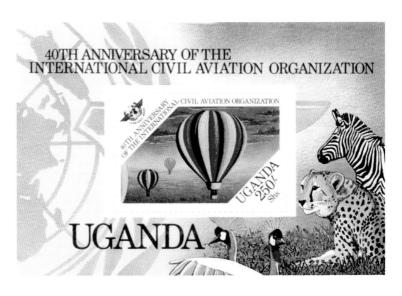

countries have been on the well-trodden tourist-trail for some time and now Uganda is becoming increasingly popular and notwithstanding the poor road infrastructure aviation is stepping in and this series of stamps really give a good insight into the country and its aviation in 1984.

Ethiopia lies to the north west of Uganda on our adventure in Africa, in a region known as the Horn of Africa – a glance at a map will show why. In the late nineteenth-century Scramble for Africa, Ethiopia was one of only two nations to retain its sovereignty from long-term colonialism by a European power but was occupied by Italy in 1936 and became Italian Ethiopia until 1947. Some of the oldest skeletal evidence for anatomically modern humans has been found in Ethiopia. It is widely considered as the region from which modern humans

first set out for the Middle East and places beyond. Today, the country is more often remembered for the awful droughts and starvation suffered.

Ethiopian Airlines was first formed late in 1945 and began commercial services the following year so this series of stamps issued in 1955 marks the first decade and shows Emperor Haile Selassie who came to power after Independence.

Initial aircraft were Douglas C-47 or DC-3 aircraft but here we see Convair CV-240, a very early post-war airliner from the USA that could carry up to forty passengers. The airline has continued to grow until today it is Africa's largest with a very modern fleet expanding to all quarters of the globe and the next set gives a chronological series of illustrations from those initial C-47s right up to the present day's Boeing 787 Dreamliner. (Currency in Ethiopia is the Birr, divided into 100 santim)

ASIA

sia is the largest continent, stretching from the Urals and the Red Sea across to eastern China, Japan, the Philippines and Singapore. Of that, two countries in this book, Russia and Turkey, have been dealt with in Chapter 3; the Russian capital is in Europe, whilst Turkey's capital Istanbul where the Bosphorus separates Europe from Asia Minor, a peninsula also called Anatolia, comprises most of the Asian part of modern Turkey and the Armenian highland, so that leaves this chapter slightly short, but nevertheless ...

Saudi Arabia has its western shore alongside the Red Sea that separates Africa from Asia. It is a desert country encompassing most of the Arabian Peninsula and known as the birthplace of Islam and home to the religion's two most sacred mosques: Masjid al-Haram, in Mecca, destination of the annual Hajj pilgrimage; and Medina's

Masjid an-Nabawi, burial site of the prophet Muhammad. Riyadh, the capital, is a skyscraper-filled metropolis.

It is the world's second largest producer of petroleum and is a Unitary Islamic totalitarian absolute monarchy retaining a very insular attitude, hence commercial aviation has never been a major priority. Things are changing slowly and this pane of four stamps from 2004 illustrates some of the modern jets in use at the time.

Pakistan. As a result of the Partition of India in 1947, the largely Muslim-populated areas became Pakistan whilst the mainly Hindu-populated areas remained in India. That meant that the Muslim community was spilt in two, in the north-west was West Pakistan whilst to the north-east of the Indian Sub-continent it was East Pakistan, although in 1971 this area separated to become Bangladesh.

Pakistan has since flourished as a nation and its own airline PIA was established in 1955 as an amalgam of several smaller carriers, and today serves domestic and international destinations world-wide including being the first non-communist carrier to serve China in 1964.

This single stamp from 1980 celebrates the 25th Anniversary of PIA and as well as the DC-3 then used on domestic services, shows a Boeing 747-200 'Jumbo-Jet' of which the country and airline were immensely proud. It wasn't all plain-sailing and the airline found great difficulties maintaining these and later 747-300 aircraft and has now replaced them all with new-build Boeing 777s twin-jets.

Continued tensions in the area have meant that defence issues have always been to the fore and this next stamp was issued on the 75th Anniversary of the No.6

Air Transport Support Squadron, Pakistan Air Force, and therein lies an enigma.

The country wasn't established until 1947 and it took a lot of digging to establish that the squadron was originally part of the Indian Air Force, much revered, then as now. It was established in 1942 at Trichinopoly and equipped with Hawker Hurricane FR. IIb aircraft. On 15 February 1944, Flying Officer J.C. Verma of the Squadron shot down a Japanese fighter during a low-level dogfight, making him the first Indian pilot since the First World War with a confirmed victory in air combat while flying for the Indian Air Force, and was decorated with the Distinguished Flying Cross. One aircraft that rarely finds itself the subject of aviation stamps is the blunt-nosed Bristol B.170 Mk.31 Freighter, surely not the most beautiful or charismatic of aircraft but obviously sufficiently rated to deserve a place here.

India is a vast South Asian country with diverse terrain – from Himalayan peaks to Indian Ocean coastline – and history reaching back five millennia. In the north, Mughal Empire landmarks include Delhi's Red Fort complex and massive Jama Masjid mosque, plus Agra's iconic Taj Mahal mausoleum. Pilgrims bathe in the Ganges in Varanasi, and Rishikesh is a yoga centre and base for Himalayan trekking.

Aviation was slow to start and it was to be 1932 before Tata Airlines was formed and was later to become Air India.

In this stamp we see that first aircraft – a de Havilland DH.80 Puss Moth – with its pilot and founder, Jehangir Ratanji Dadabhoy Tata (1904-93), a French-born Indian aviator, entrepreneur, chairman of Tata Group and the shareholder of Tata Sons. Researchers should be aware! Obviously held in high esteem, this little aircraft first appeared on another stamp in 1979. Whilst in Britain registration marks remain unique and never used again, in India that is not the case and this particular one has since been used again at least one, for an ATR 42 turbo-prop commuter aircraft.

Air India's first flight to the UK was operated by Lockheed Constellations in 1948 and this very traditional monochrome stamp issued that year reminds us of how a great many of the world's stamps appeared in that era.

By contrast, this 2005 image celebrates another squadron's anniversary much as we saw under the Pakistani heading, and here we see interesting illustrations of three noteworthy aircraft: from the '60s – a SEPECAT (Société Européenne de Production de l'avion Ecole de

Combat et d'Appui Tactique) Jaguar Attack Aircraft, a joint venture between Breguet in France and the British Aircraft Corporation, and still in use in India: from the '40s and '50s an English Electric Canberra light bomber and from the Second World War era a Consolidated B-24 Liberator 4-engined heavy bomber.

Coming forward to 2012, this interesting view reminds us that India today retains strong trading ties with Russia and thus buys their aircraft from the east as well as from the West. Shown here is an Ilyushin IL-76MD, an Airborne Warning and Control System aircraft more readily known in the west by the acronym AWACS. The IL-76 is a 4-engined freighter first-flown in 1971 and apparently still in production in up-graded form with almost 1,000 produced – so far.

China is separated from India to the south by the Himalayan Mountain Range, a formidable obstacle to both trade and confrontation until aviation developed sufficiently to get across the colossal heights. From being one of the world's earliest civilizations, China has grown to be the world's most populous country, with a population of around 1.4 billion in 2017 and a land area of close to 10 million square kilometres, behind Russia and Canada. Before the economic reforms in 1978, China had been an extremely insular nation and aviation was not a significant priority, Commercial aviation was minimalist and undertaken by the state run CAAC (Civil Aviation Administration of China) whilst its military flying was undertaken by PLAAF (The People's Liberation Army Air Force), a branch of the People's Liberation Army, the armed forces of the People's Republic of China. The PLAAF was officially established on 11 November 1949 with a rudimentary fleet that today has grown to around 400,000 personnel and is the largest air force in Asia.

Deng Xiaoping took power in 1978 and instituted significant economic reforms. The Communist Party

loosened governmental control over citizens' personal lives, and the communes were gradually disbanded. This marked China's transition from a planned economy to a mixed economy with an increasingly open-market environment. Since then of course the nation and its economy has flourished and what was the issue of infrequent stamps on aviation subjects is now beginning to produce some very attractive work.

My research (with no knowledge of the Chinese language) shows that the stamp shown, of 2003, is believed to be a Chengdu J9 fighter aircraft of 1975.

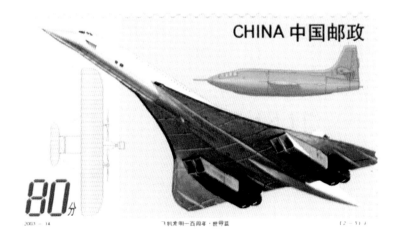

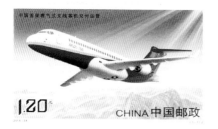

Then there are the unmistakable images of Concorde and the Chengdu J10, a multi-role medium-weight fighter.

The Changhe Z-8 is a Chinese copy of the Aerospatiale (formerly Sud Aviation) SA 321 Super Frelon.

The next is a Xian JH-7, the Flying Leopard, and finally comes the Comac C919, a narrow-body twinjet airliner developed by Chinese aerospace manufacturer Comac. The programme was launched in 2008 and production of the prototype began in December 2011. It rolled out on 2 November 2015 and first flew on 5 May 2017. The C919 is planned to enter commercial service in 2021 with China Eastern Airlines. A final note regarding these designations that are national markings rather than those of the manufacturer; J signifies a fighter aircraft; Z a helicopter; JH a fighter-bomber; and C commercial aircraft.

Hong Kong is an autonomous territory, and former British colony, in south-eastern China. Its vibrant, densely populated urban centre is a major port and global financial hub with a skyscraper-studded skyline. The territory was returned to China when the lease expired in 1997.

Apart from flights to and from the Territory, Hong Kong developed as a very busy hub in global aviation, the more so before modern aircraft were able to fly non-stop for almost 10,000miles!

This beautiful 1984 set shows us some of Hong Kong's aviation history and apart from the eponymous Boeing 747

'Jumbo Jet' treats us to images of the Sikorsky S-42B flying boat of Pan Am and a de Havilland DH-86 Dragon Express (a four-engined and enlarged version of the DH-84 Dragon and predecessor of the better known DH-86 Dragon Rapide) of Imperial Airways. We also have a 1891 balloon marked Baldwin Brothers who were early aviators in the US but I can find no references of their adventures in Hong Kong!

Korea is a peninsular to the east of the Chinese mainland that has been fought-over for millennia and today is unhappily split in two since the pro- and anti- staggered to a stalemate in 1953 but without a formalized peace treaty and ever since then an uneasy cease-fire has created greater peace than the area has ever known with the southern section, south of the 38th Parallel known as South Korea that prospers under the bountiful shadow of the US. To the north, the DPRK or Democratic People's Republic of Korea in total contrast lives under the

Communist ideology of its neighbour and friend China. As I write this a faint glimmer of hope for rapprochement is in the air, so there is hope.

Many stamps have been issued by the DPRK including these fine examples issued in 1978 and 1987 that are, should one say a little fanciful; however, the illustration of a Tupolev TU-154 in the colours of Air Koryo reminds us that in the twenty-first century the airline is still believed to be operating the type as well as Illyushin IL-62M 4-engined jet and various other, smaller Soviet types.

Indo China is a geographical term originating in the early nineteenth century and referring to the continental

portion of the region now known as Southeast Asia. The name refers to the lands historically within the cultural influence of India and China, and physically bound by the Indian Subcontinent in the west and China in the north. It corresponds to the present-day areas of Cambodia,

Thailand, Laos, Myanmar, Vietnam. The term was later adopted as the name of the colony of French Indochina (today's Cambodia, Vietnam, and Laos), and these stamps come from this era.

Vietnam has been fought over for more than a millennium; the final protagonists were the French and finally the Americans that supported the southern part of the country against the Communist Viet-Cong from the north. I have found these stamps issued by the north in this conflict to be almost unique in celebrating various victories over their hated southern neighbours and their supporters – the USA.

The Communist armies eventually overran the south in 1975 to re-unify the country and in 1986 the Communist Party of Vietnam (CPV)

initiated a series of economic and political reforms that began Vietnam's path toward integration into the world economy.

Today, under a stable administration Vietnam has blossomed into a beautiful country beloved of tourists who also talk of hugely friendly people and wonderful food.

Cambodia is another beautiful country sadly racked by conflict over the centuries and its name has varied depending upon influences internal and external, hence the stamps we see here bear the name 'Cambodge' reflecting the French influences whilst 'Kampuchea' came into use from 1975-79 when the country was under the control of the Khmer Rouge an ultra-Communist ideology. Although the official language of Cambodia is Khmer, postage stamps continued to bear the title Cambodge until well into the twenty-first century.

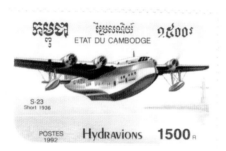

There have been many stamps issued by Cambodia illustrating transport subjects and I have chosen examples from two sets, the first from 1992 titled *hydravions* to maintain the French influence, flying boats or sea-planes in the English speaking world.

From a 1996 issue we see some rather finely detailed illustrations of earlier aircraft including a Pitcairn PS-5 Mailwing of 1926 and a Stearman C-3MB of 1927, both manufacturers being long defunct pioneers from the USA.

Thailand is known for tropical beaches, opulent royal palaces, ancient ruins and ornate temples displaying

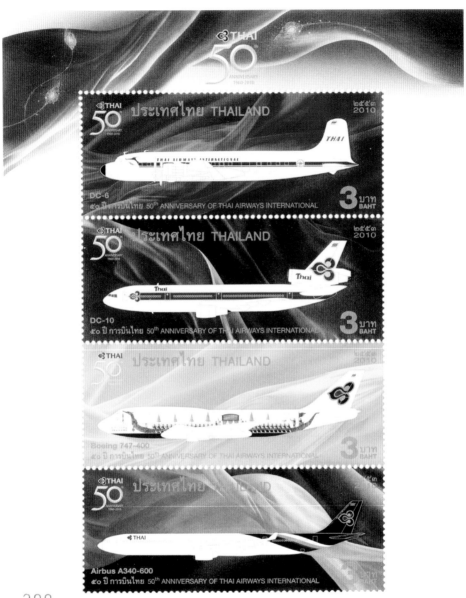

289

figures of Buddha. Bangkok is the capital, rather better known for cityscapes like the world-over – skyscrapers. Thankfully the country, until 1932 known as Siam, has avoided the colonisation and extreme bloodletting of many of its neighbours although internal politics have sometimes seemed a bit excitable!

This pane was issued in 2010 to celebrate the 50th anniversary of Thai International Airlines and illustrates some of the history of this relatively young airline formed in 1960 with the help of the Scandinavian Airlines System (SAS). The first aircraft shown, a Douglas DC-6, clearly shows its origins with the Viking motif of SAS whilst later stamps give an impression of the beautiful artistry that forms a significant part of the nation's heritage.

Malasia is south of the Indo-China region and in the Malay Peninsular consisting of 13 states and three federal territories, separated by the South China Sea into two similarly sized regions, Peninsular Malaysia and East Malaysia (Malaysian Borneo). Its history has been a complicated one including British rule and only in 1963 was Malaya united with North Borneo, Sarawak, and Singapore to become Malaysia although Singapore subsequently seceded to go its own way.

The three stamps were issued in 1997 to mark fifty years of aviation in the country showing with pride the elegant Boeing 747 'Jumbo Jet' to which at the time every international airline aspired. Interestingly we also see the tail of a short-lived Malaysia Singapore Airlines jet.

In 2007 this little set illustrates some aircraft less-frequently seen on stamps but used for short-distance and internal use: The Shorts SC.7 Skyvan produced in Northern Islands, the GAF 22 Nomad from Australia and the de Havilland Canada DHC7 4-engined turboprop aircraft famed for its extremely short take-off and landing capabilities.

Singapore was founded by Stamford Raffles in 1819 as a trading post of the British East India Company. After the company's collapse in 1858, the islands were ceded to the British Raj as a crown colony. During the Second World War, Singapore was occupied by Japan. It gained independence from the UK in 1963 by federating with other former British territories to form Malaysia, but separated two years later over ideological differences, becoming a sovereign nation in 1965. After early years of turbulence and despite lacking natural resources and a hinterland, the nation developed rapidly as an Asian Tiger economy.

When, in 2003, Singapore issued a set of 20 stamps to mark the centenary of powered flight, they were also produced as a mini-sheet (sic) that I find impossible to ignore. Although extremely attractive stamps, the set oddly omits anything but products of the modern era!

The country's national airline Singapore Airlines has consistently been cited as one of, if not the world's favourite airline for the quality of its service and had the privilege of operating the world's first commercial flight of the Airbus 380 airliner. Unlike the Boeing 747 that quickly gained the nickname 'Jumbo Jet', the A380 has never had such a moniker, sometimes being referred to as the 'super-jumbo' or 'whale' to emphasise its almost unimaginable size. Here we see a special cover issued to mark the occasion with a stamp.

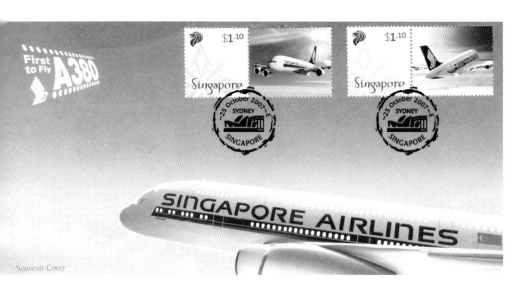

Souvenir Cover

AUSTRALIA, NEW ZEALAND AND THE PACIFIC REGION

Australia Think kangaroos, koalas, the Sydney Harbour Bridge and the adjacent Opera House. The country is treated as a continent in its own right and other than native Aborigines was first colonised by Europeans from England and was used for many years as a penal colony for criminals that were sentenced to be

'transported' to Australia. Today it is inhabited primarily by English speaking peoples that can still trace their origins back to the United Kingdom and the country retains its ties with the UK as a member of the British Commonwealth with HM the Queen as its Head of State. It is sometimes difficult to appreciate the size of the world's biggest island but to help one should first imagine the distance from London to Glasgow at roughly 400 miles or 640 kilometres whilst Sydney to Melbourne (in the bottom right hand corner of the continent) is 550 miles or 880 Kilometres, and Brisbane to Perth right across the continent from east to west is 2,250 miles or 3,610 kilometres with the vast majority of land between consisting of desert.

Aviation has played an important part in the development of the country, both internally and in connecting with 'the mother country' and shown here is the first stamp from this country to feature aviation – a 1929 monochrome image so typical of the era, and featuring a de Havilland D.H.66 Hercules of Western Australian Airways and marked for Air Mail post.

This mini-sheet graphically illustrates this latter aspect, the Shorts S.30 'Empire' Flying boat of the immediate post Second World War era, the name QANTAS is still with us today and originally stood for Queensland And Northern Territories Air Service. Note also the transition from the early UK-legacy currency to Australia's own dollars and cents that was effected in 1966.

This particular stamp was one of a set of four stamps issued in 2008 and seen in a little presentation pack, to coincide with the introduction to service of the Airbus A.380 airliner, the world's largest, carrying 450 passengers and with the announcement in February 2019 that manufacturing of the type would cease with completion of current orders it seems likely to retain is accolade of the world's largest for the foreseeable future.

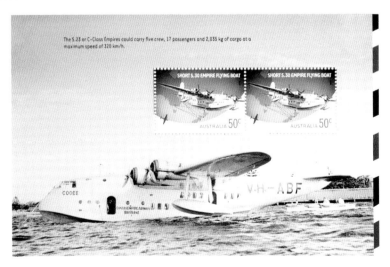

The Bristol Tourer was a rugged and dependable aircraft chosen to undertake the Federal Government's first airmail and passenger service in 1921. No less elegant in the set are the elegant lines of the Lockheed L1049 Super Constellation of 1954 that operated all of Qantas's international services until the arrival of the Boeing 707 in 1959

Australia's military services are celebrated in this issue from 1996 and apart from illustrating aircraft old and new we are treated in the gutter to the insignia each of the nation's forces; at each end is the Australian Defence Force whilst within are the insignia of the Navy, Army and Air Force.

And if what you want is colourful stamps this set of stamps from 2008 is for you and coincides with the 150th anniversary of the first hot-air balloon flight in Australia. Surely here we have the most iconic view of the country – the Sydney Harbour Bridge and the Sydney Opera House.

These two final stamps from 1973 reminds us that Australia is in the Southern Hemisphere and not all that far from Antarctica. Like several other nations Australia maintains a presence in that region and accordingly issues appropriate stamps. The 8c stamp shows a D.H.83 Fox

Moth and the 35c Avro 581 Avion both flown by notable Australian Polar Explorers.

Fiji is in an area of the Southern Pacific known as Melanesia to the east of Australia and together with Polynesia dotted with hundreds of small islands as well as the larger ones of New Zealand. Palm trees, endless white sandy beaches and grass skirts immediately come to mind but long before the era of long-distance tourism many of them built-up their economies based on local resources and in the 400 or so islands that formed the archipelago of Fiji, it was sugar cane.

The islands were annexed by the British in 1874 but that succeeded in introducing measles into the country that cost the lives of over 40,000 Fijians, or one third of the native population! Early stamps also came from UK printers and exhibited all the trade-marks one would expect – intricate framing, the monarch's head and of course, UK-based currency. They were at least produced in two colours and this one illustrated the early airport of the capital Nadi (pronounced Nandi).

Independence came in 1970 and with it a change of currency to local dollars and cents although the islands have not enjoyed a settled government since.

This set of stamps illustrates design influences still largely from the UK and marks the 25th anniversary of air services in these islands, the de Havilland Australia D.H.A.3 Drover in particular being interesting as an adaptation to Australian conditions of the two-engined British de Havilland Dove mini-airliner.

Finally a particularly attractive stamp shows one of many post Second World War light aircraft that took their cue from communications aircraft used by the US where Taylorcraft was started in the 1930s by a Briton Charles G. Taylor and his designs were developed in both the US and the UK by such well-known names as Piper and Auster. Aeronca was another such manufacturer in the US and they produced the aptly named L-3 Grasshopper seen here in its natural environment.

Nouvelle Caledonie got its first title New Caledonia thanks to the British explorer James Cook who found much to remind him of Scotland. However in 1853, the

French took control of the territory comprising dozens of islands in the Melanesia region of the South Pacific. Like most of the South Pacific region it is known for its palm-lined beaches and marine-life-rich lagoon, which, at 24,000sq. km is among the world's largest. A massive barrier reef surrounds the main island, Grand Terre, a major scuba-diving destination. The capital, Nouméa, is home to French-influenced restaurants and luxury boutiques selling Parisian fashions. Currency has always been French centimes and francs.

Postage stamps here like those from all French colonies bear the initials 'RF' for Republique Français, and this first illustrated from 1983 also bears all the hallmarks of French design and taste. It shows the ill-starred but hugely

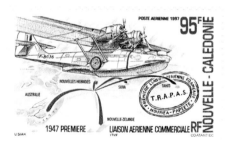

popular Mignet MH.14 Pou de Ciel, a name that translates literally as Sky Louse although I believe that at the time the contemporary vernacular was referring to a Flying Flea!. First flown in 1933, unfortunately the design proved very difficult to fly for its intended market – the amateur builder and pilot – and many was the swift end for both aircraft and aviator. Even in the twenty-first century efforts to redesign the aircraft have had only moderate success.

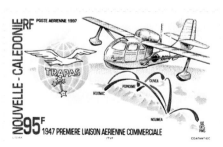

Moving forward to 1997 we see stamps illustrating route maps of TRAPAS (les TRansports Aériens du PAcifique Sud), an airline that operated from 1946-51 using amphibious aircraft such as the well-known Consolidated PBY-5 Catalina, originally designed as a wartime search and rescue craft and the smaller Republic Rc-3 Seabee seaplane.

Vanuatu's story parallels that of New Caledonia in many ways as it too is an archipelago in the Melanesia area of the South Pacific that was named the Hebrides Scottish Archipelago by early settlers including James Cook, but here British and French colonialists chose to share responsibilities as a Condominium until, following a brief 'Coconut War', independence was achieved in 1980.

Like many aspects of life at that time, postage stamps were issued by each power until towards the end of the colonial days joint issues began to appear and here the first series of stamps is a wonderful example of the shared power – the

1994 C&O AIR VANUATU BOEING 737
International Civil Aviation Organisation 1944-1994

1966 NEW HEBRIDES AIRWAYS DROVER
International Civil Aviation Organisation 1944-1994

1956 TAI DOUGLAS DC3
International Civil Aviation Organisation 1944-1994

1950 QANTAS CATALINA
International Civil Aviation Organisation 1944-1994

French *and* British monograms given equal prominence whilst aircraft from both countries' manufacturers are tactfully included. As one might expect, aviation has played an important role in countries like this separated by great distances from major land masses and so they appear frequently on stamps. Independence, with the name Vanuato, here didn't change things and this set from 1994, ostensibly to celebrate the 50th anniversary of ICAO (International Civil Aviation Organisation), does show rather nicely the characteristic nature of these islands.

New Zealand Sometime between 1250 and 1300, Polynesians settled in the islands that later were named New Zealand and developed a distinctive Māori culture. In 1642, the Dutch became the first Europeans to see what they named New Zealand. In 1840, representatives of the United Kingdom and Māori chiefs signed the Treaty of Waitangi declaring British sovereignty over the islands becoming a colony within the British Empire and in 1907 becoming a Dominion. It gained full statutory independence in 1947 and the British monarch remains head of state. Today, roughly 75 per cent of the inhabitants are of European ancestry.

The main islands and hundreds of smaller ones are actually in the Polynesian section of the South Pacific but being so far south of other countries in the same area and closer to the Antarctic its climate is considered temperate, very much like that of the UK which probably explains its attraction to British immigrants.

Like so many other countries that are isolated from other great land-masses, New Zealand developed commercial air routes quite early-on to connect with fellow Commonwealth countries and establish air-mail services and this 1955 stamp is typical of the conventional stamp of the era and showing a Douglas DC-3 usually and

universally known as a Dakota although this is not an official designation.

Heritage is taken very seriously in New Zealand where there are a great many elderly types restored to flying condition. In this set are some very fine examples including

an indigenous Fletcher FU24 Topdresser that first flew in 1954 and one of 297 built.

And lastly, the 75 years of international flying by Air New Zealand and its predecessor Tasman Empire Airways Ltd

(TEAL) is told in words and photographs by this set of stamps issued in 2015.

Tonga For those readers who recall the coronation of HM Queen Elizabeth II in 1953 one endearing memory will be of the Tongan Queen Salote who defied the miserable rain on the day by travelling in an open carriage and waving to the crowds out on The Mall and in front of Buckingham Palace. In a similar spirit, when the Tongan athlete Pita Taufatofua led his nation's team in the opening parade of the 2016 Rio Olympics he was an unknown, unrated athlete from an obscure Pacific island but quickly became a global celebrity. Had it not been for a vat of coconut oil, a straw skirt and his flair for flag bearing, he could have passed through the Olympic Games unnoticed and unreported. As it was his story went viral!

Such stories mark the Tongan people as special and made it difficult for me to disregard this small series of 170 islands and their stamps. In characteristic Polynesian and South Pacific fashion most of these islands are noted for their luxurious beaches and palm trees, it is an independent island nation located approximately 400 miles (approximately 650km) southeast of Fiji and roughly 1150 miles (1850km) northeast of New Zealand. Tonga is the only remaining Polynesian monarchy. Nuku'alofa is the country's capital, chief port, and largest town.

As early as 1979 Tonga was issuing self-adhesive stamps and these were also an early example of individualism by making them 'cloud' shape!

This 1982 issue marked the inauguration of Nuku'alofa International Airport whilst South Pacific Island Airways was an operator based in Honolulu and that operated from 1973-87. The currency used is 100 Seniti = 1 Pa'anga.

I mentioned in the opening remarks of the Introduction that I'd come across a perplexing stamp bearing the inscription Niuafo'ou, Kingdom of Tonga. Google Translate was no help but Wikipedia explained that it is the most northerly island in the kingdom of Tonga and its name translates as 'Many New Coconuts' or 'Tin Can Island' (One takes one's choice!) It is a volcanic rim island with an area of 15sq.km and a population of 650 in 2006.

THE AMERICAS

Canada is second only to Russia in land area – 9.985 million sq.km compared to 17.1 million sq.km. Like Russia too, large swathes of the country are pretty desolate, cold and isolated; hence aviation played an early part in developing these areas and providing on-going connectivity. Today, Canada is a parliamentary democracy and a constitutional monarchy, with Queen Elizabeth II being the head of state. The country is a realm within the Commonwealth of Nations.

Canada also shares a unique situation with another far-off country, this time New Hebrides – or as it is now known Vanuatu – and that is colonisation by both the British and French, and whilst Vanuatu has now shed all formal ties with its colonial developers, in Canada the two influences continue to happily live side by side and whilst the official language in most of the country is English, the province of Quebec still maintains French as its official language and strong ties with its 'mother-country'. Expect to find much of the county's formal documents produced in both languages, and that includes postage stamps too.

These three early examples illustrate the importance of air-mail. The 6c example from 1928 shows a rare case where the stamp has subsequently been over-printed with an up-dated value before issue (an early example of inflation?) whilst the 17c value from 1942 which shows a Lockheed

L-18 Lodestar given the appearance of speed is produced to reflect the extra cost necessary for the speediest service whilst the 7c stamp is of the same year at a standard price.

From 1979 to '82 the Canadian Post issued a small series showing some of the aeronautical products of the country whether home-grown or licence built. Some well-known names in British manufacturing including Avro and de Havilland are shown and whilst the former thrived for many years in Canada, its choice of the ever-expanding cost of military types eventually led to its downfall in 1962. De Havilland, however, was more fortunate and after aircraft such as the Chipmunk Trainer, the Beaver and Otter utility aircraft, the company developed the short-haul passenger types such as the four-engined DHC7 and more recently the DHC-8 that is still in production today under the successor organisation Bombardier.

We have more very attractive stamps, this time showing the 'Snowbirds', a flight of Canadair CT-114 Tutors and Canada's answer to the UK's Red Arrows and from the US the 'Thunderbirds'.

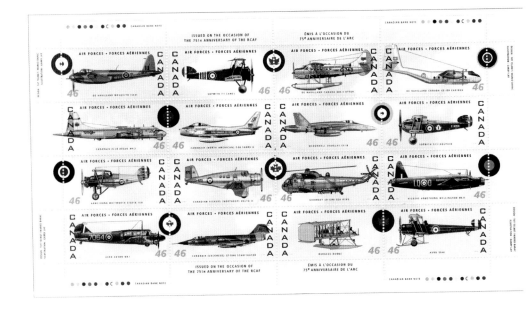

In 1999, Canada Post issued this set of no less than sixteen stamps to celebrate the 75th anniversary of the RCAF, the Royal Canadian Air Force. Technically, this pane of stamps should be referred to as a mini-sheet but could almost be classed as suitable for framing.

The United States of America has to be *the* pre-eminent manufacturer of the world's aviation, be it civil or military. Although rather diminished in terms of major airliner manufacturers to but one name – Boeing – others such as Lockheed-Martin continue in the military field and these and their contemporaries produce in prodigious quantities bolstered by the huge

demand for passenger travel and of course the insatiable appetite for military hardware from both home and abroad.

Of course for powered, heavier-than-air flight it all started in a field four miles south of Kitty Hawk, North

Carolina on 17 December 1903 and two brothers called Orville and Wilbur Wright and surprisingly quickly brave individuals like William Frederick 'Buffalo Bill' Cody joined in with barn-storming flying circuses and then carrying mail throughout the country before passenger flights (for the brave!) started on 1 January 1914 between St Petersburg and Tampa, Florida.

The first stamps to feature aircraft was in 1918 but I have chosen this stamp, on the previous page, to start with, issued in 1927 to mark Charles Lindbergh's epic first solo flight across the Atlantic on 21 May of that year. So much of this stamp marks the fashion of the era – a monochrome illustration with embellishments that have the look of contemporary bank notes and stock certificates.

Coming forward to 1947, the world was still recovering from the distresses of the Second World War, so this stamp shows none of the frivolity we expect from American stamps, but it is a fine view of a modern airliner of the day – a Lockheed Constellation – with a background view of the iconic

Igor Sikorsky

Manhattan skyscraper skyline and the Statue of Liberty. Like so many stamps featuring aircraft, this one is inscribed 'Air Mail' to reflect the supplemental charge for the service.

Many stamps issued throughout the world feature great pioneers and the USA is no exception. A particularly good example comes from 1988 and shows Igor Sikorsky together with his first helicopter – the Vought-Sikorsky VS.300. Igor Ivanovich Sikorsky was born in Kiev (now in Ukraine) in 1889 and from an early age was fascinated by all things mechanical and in particular aviation. It is said that whilst at Kiev University he experimented with the concept of helicopters and built a model powered by rubber-bands.

He later set up a very successful aircraft manufacturing business in Russia but with the Bolshevik Revolution that started in 1917 he fled his homeland, first to France and then in 1919 to America where he quickly

re-established himself as a manufacturer of both fixed-wing aircraft and then helicopters. He is generally acknowledged as being the inventor of the modern-day machine if one is to except earlier experiments by the French and Germans, and of course the genius brain of da Vinci. Although the business later became part of the giant United Aircraft and Transport Corporation, his name lives on with every helicopter the business produces today.

Moving forward to 1997, the US Postal Service issued no less than twenty stamps valued at 32c and showing some of the country's aviation manufacturers' well known products of the immediate post-war years and I have chosen to show just seven here.

Finally, here is a cover produced independently to mark the 40th anniversary of the world's first commercial round-the-world service. The painting by John Young of the Guild of Aviation Artists is sufficient qualification to appear here showing the Boeing B314 'Yankee Clipper' flying boat and operated by Pan American Airways, known to everyone as

On 2nd December, 1941, Capt Robert Ford flew Boeing B-314, NC 18603 "Yankee Clipper" from San Francisco to New York on a westerly route round the world, landing in New York on 6th January, 1942.

This cover was carried by courtesy of Pan American World Airways over the following route :—

30.12.81	London — San Francisco. Boeing 747.	
	Capt. A. S. Wilson. Flt Time: 10hrs 30mins.	
31.12.81	San Francisco — Honolulu. Boeing 747.	
	Capt. D. Parsons, Flt Time: 5hrs 30mins.	
31.12.81	Honolulu — Auckland. Boeing 747.	
	Capt. C. H. Stewart. Flt Time: 8hrs 29mins.	
2.1.82	Auckland — Honolulu. Boeing 747.	
	Capt. R. Flinn. Flt Time: 8hrs 10mins.	
2.1.82	Honolulu — Tokyo. Boeing 747.	
	Capt. R. Thompson. Flt Time: 8hrs 25mins.	
4.1.82	Tokyo — New York. Boeing 747.	
	Capt. R. A. Peters. Flt Time: 14hrs.	
7.1.82	New York — Los Angeles. Boeing 747.	
	Capt. A. Wicksman. Flt Time: 5hrs 50mins.	
10.1.82	Los Angeles — London. Boeing 747.	
	Capt. R. Loomis. Flt Time: 10hrs 15mins.	
	Courier T. Treadwell, R.A.F. Museum.	

Pan Am. The USA never had a state-owned commercial airline, preferring to allow private enterprise to lead the way even if sometimes they were subsidised under the umbrella of air-mail contracts, and Pan Am became the leading airline on international routes from the very earliest days. Having used flying boats manufactured by Sikorsky, Boeing became the preferred supplier, thanks in no small way to the personal contact between the two concerns' senior management, so Pan Am became lead buyer for such aircraft as the B.377 Stratocruiser, the B.707 4-engined jet and finally the B.747 'Jumbo Jet' that single-handedly introduced air-travel to the masses.

Tragically, Pan Am was unable to adapt successfully to a changing aviation world of de-regulation and eventually succumbed in December 1991, a very sad loss of a wonderful institution.

Mexico On our journey south through the Americas, Mexico is the first country we come to in what is generally called Central America, that relatively thin strip of land that connects North and South America. Also, it is the northern-most country in the region referred to as Latin America, generally understood to consist of the entire continent of South America, Central America, and the islands of the Caribbean whose inhabitants speak a Romance language. The peoples of this large area shared the experience of conquest and colonization by the Spaniards and Portuguese from the late fifteenth through to the eighteenth century. In Mexico, the language spoken by the vast majority of the population is Spanish, a throw-back to Spanish colonisation and the Viceroyalty of New Spain in 1535. The Mexican postal system has its roots in the Aztec system of messengers which the Spanish adopted after the Conquest. A postal service was established in 1580, mainly to communicate between the Viceroyalty of New Spain with the motherland Spain.

In 2010 the current postal service – Sepomex – (Servicio Postal Mexicano) issued a large series of stamps to

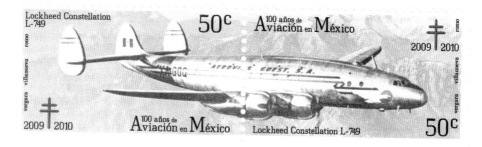

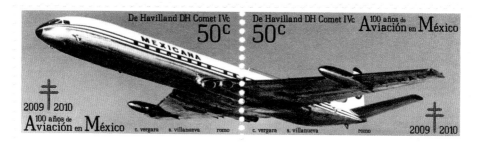

celebrate a centenary of aviation in the country and I have chosen these stamps to illustrate them and show current operator Areonaves de Mexico, now more generally known as Aeromexico, and Mexicana that ceased operations in 2010.

Cuba is the largest of the Caribbean Islands that sit uncomfortably between North and South America. With its capital of Havana, Cuba is well known today for its Communist affiliations that followed the Cuban Revolution of 1959 and which has held the island's economy back generations, preserved 1950s cars in

everyday use and almost caused a nuclear conflict in the Cuban Crisis of 1962.

Like many similar countries, Cuba has used its postage stamps as a mark of the pride the country has for the

areas where progress has been made and one such area is aviation where principally Soviet-manufactured equipment has given the country access to the outside world denied to it by the US-led embargos. I have picked stamps from three different issues to show some of the highlights, in the pre-communist era of premiere Fidel Castro.

American types were a natural choice and here was see a Ford Tri-motor and Sikorsky S-38B flying boat from the late 1920s, and a Lockheed Constellation and Douglas DC-6 from the early 50s.

As the embargo began to bite, the national airline Cubana turned to the UK for five Bristol Britannia 300s to be followed by Soviet-era machines such as the Ilyushin IL-62 and Il-96 four-engined jets, the latter remaining in use to connect with Russia into the twenty-first century.

Colombia is one of the more northerly countries of South America. The Spanish arrived in 1499 and hence the country adopted their language like many others in the region. Independence came in 1819 although it was to be 1886 before the Republic was finally formed.

The country has issued many aviation related stamps since its first in 1932 and interestingly quite a few such as this one from 1969 illustrate the Junkers F-13 seaplane, the first aircraft to be used as a mail plane in 1919. The second stamp in this particular issue shows a Boeing 720B belonging to the national airline Avianca, a foreshortened version of the famous 707, produced as many airlines at that time were cautious of the high capacity of the latter even though by then the jumbo 747 was already flying. Avianca SA (acronym in Spanish for 'Aerovías del Continente Americano S.A.', Airways of the American Continent) was established in 1919 as

the country's flag carrier and today remains a very major player in South American commercial aviation although now privatised.

Ecuador, as its name suggests sits on the Equator and is a coastal country with a northern border with Colombia. Its diverse landscape encompasses Amazon jungle, Andean highlands and the wildlife-rich Galápagos Islands. In the Andean foothills at an elevation of 2,850m, Quito, the capital, is known for its largely intact Spanish colonial centre with decorated sixteenth- and seventeenth-century palaces and religious sites, like the ornate Compañía de Jesús Church. Quito is also the world's second highest capital city after La Paz, Bolivia.

Tame (pronounced 'tah-meh') is the nation's flag carrier formed in 1962 by the Air Force of Ecuador to serve smaller and more remote areas. In 2011, it became a state-owned commercial entity and now provides domestic, international and charter flights.

Since 1986 Avianca of Colombia has been a significant commercial operator in Ecuador so

this series of stamps issued in 1988 to mark the 60th anniversary of Avianca's operation in the country, is a veritable history of the airline from the Junkers F-13 already seen on Colombia's stamps and the Dornier Wal twin-engined flying boat through to a Boeing 727 tri-jet in Avianca's modern red livery.

Brazil moves us to the east side of the continent with a long Atlantic shoreline. It is a huge country, stretching from the Amazon Basin in the north to vineyards and massive Iguaçu Falls in the south. Rio de Janeiro, symbolized by its 38m high Christ the Redeemer statue atop Mount Corcovado, is famed for its busy Copacabana and Ipanema beaches as well as its enormous, raucous *Carnaval* festival, featuring parade floats, flamboyant costumes, samba music and dance.

Brazilians speak Portuguese as their principal language that dates back to Portuguese colonisation starting in 1500; the Brazilian War of Independence brought it to an end in 1824. Today Brazil has the largest economy of Latin America and a significant proportion of this is represented by aviation. Embraer, that today ranks as the world's third largest aircraft manufacturer after Boeing and Airbus, was established by the Brazilian government in

1969, formally Empresa Brasileira de Aeronáutica as a government-owned corporation that initially produced a turboprop passenger aircraft, the Embraer EMB 110 Bandeirante (Bandit).

The company was privatised in 1994 and has continued to expand in both military and civil field where the latest 195-E2 airliner is offered with seating for up to 146 passengers.

The second stamp shows an Italian Savoia Marchetti S-64 of 1928 specifically built to contest world duration and distance records. Arturo Ferrarin (1895-1941) and Carlo Del Prete (1897-1928), two Italian pioneer aviators, made one of their record breaking flights from Italy to Brazil covering a distance of a little over 5000 miles in 48 hours! Continuing the trans-Atlantic theme, these next stamps, below, mark the 50th anniversary of what was claimed to be the world's first regular trans-oceanic commercial flight, from Germany to Brazil in 1934 and using the Dornier Do-J 'Wal' (Whale) flying boat.

How wonderful it is to see a hang-glider on a postage stamp and this 1991 example, issued to mark the eighth World Free Flight Championships, is one of several issued by Correios, the Brazilian postal service.

Argentina takes up the majority of the southern part of the continent along the Atlantic Coast and shares the southern tip, including Isla Grande de Tierra del Fuego with its neighbour to the west Chile. Argentina has the world's largest Spanish-speaking population and its capital Buenos Aires translates into English as Fair Winds. One thinks of Argentina and thinks of the tango and beef.

The country has a long history of aviation and the number of stamps from this country reflect this. Its own manufacturing facility, Fábrica Argentina de Aviones SA (FAdeA), becoming Fábrica Militar de Aviones (FMA), and although privatised in the 1990s it returned to state ownership in 2009 and has been responsible for a very large number of projects although few reached double figures in numbers built, There were 120 Pucara counter-insurgency/light attack aircraft built that were seen during the Falklands War, as well as indigenous and licence-built trainers also in considerable numbers.

Aerolíneas Argentinas is Argentina's largest airline and the country's flag carrier. The airline was created in 1949 from the merger of four companies, and started operations in December 1950. Following a world-wide fashion, the airline was privatised in 1990 but having proved financially almost catastrophic it returned to State control and finally ownership as well in 2008.

The first stamp here from 1959 shows an early commitment to jet-power, in this case operating six of the de Havilland Comet 4 that marked a continuing and lucrative association with British manufacturers that was abruptly ended by the war in the Falklands in 1982.

Air Mail services were the subject of a set of stamps and include very attractive renditions of the Bleriot X1, a Junkers F-13L, a Latecoere 26, whose operations were eloquently described by the French writer Antoine de Saint-Exupéry, himself a pilot of the day in Argentina, and finally

a PBY-5A Catalina amphibian that had been used during the Second World War almost world-wide. Finally a pair of stamps featuring some of Argentina's military aviation, from 2000 another illustration of the Dornier Do-J Wal featured before whilst from 2002 another Consolidated PBY-5A Catalina being seen here supporting the country's presence in Antarctica.

The Falkland Islands I am aware that discussing these islands just after Argentina is, to say the least, unfortunate but with these islands (known to the Argentineans as Islas Malvinas) being so close – a mere 300 miles away – it is difficult to place the Falklands anywhere else in this book.

It was 1833 when the Union Flag was first staked down here although Argentina still maintains its right to sovereignty over the islands. Inhabitants (3,398 in 2016) primarily consist of native-born Falkland Islanders, the majority of British descent. Until the Argentine military invaded the Falklands in April 1982, the world knew very little of this group of islands and typical aviation was represented by this stamp of 1952 with its little Auster J/1 Autocrat, a 1940s British single-engined three-seat high-wing touring monoplane built by Auster Aircraft Limited at Rearsby, Leicestershire.

Afterwards, the UK Government threw its mighty weight against the intruders from half way around the world. Two different RAF aircraft types were especially note-worthy in the ensuing conflict:

The Harrier 'Jump Jet', originally developed by British manufacturer Hawker Siddeley in the 1960s, was a single-engined Vertical and Short take-off fighter that swivelled it exhausts more than 90 degrees from level flight to downwards and slightly forwards to effect rearward

flight. What nobody outside the squadrons' closed doors knew was the technique of 'viffing', the ability to stop – in mid-air – to the astonishment of chasing Argentinean fighters who suddenly found themselves in front of their foe, and in their gun-sights. I have been a regular reader of *The Stamp Magazine* published by the Stanley Gibbons organisation and thoroughly recommend it to budding philatelists, and in the October 2008 edition full details of the production of this stamp and the rest in the set were described. The original artwork was undertaken by Ross Watton, an accomplished artist who had actually served in the Royal Navy and is more famous for his marine work.

In 2008, a new series of definitive stamps was issued by the island which, like so many stamps issued before and after the conflict featured aircraft and one of them featured the Avro Vulcan designed as part of the Nuclear Deterrent and first flown in 1952. Contemporary to the Vulcan was the Handley Page Victor and Vickers Valiant – henceforth known as the V-Force – but none of them ever operated in anger until two Vulcans left their UK base with conventional bombs to put the Falklands' only airstrip out of action in one of the RAF's most audacious and complex operations. The operation needed support from several H.P. Victors converted to K2 in-flight tanker configuration, several of which required tanker-to-tanker refuelling. One Vulcan succeeded in its task and thus entered the island's folklore.

THE PHILATELIST

As with the Introduction, this section is included in all books in this series as it is expected that each will appeal to a different audience. To those that see this again – we request your forbearance.

COLLECTING

What makes us collect stamps? Come to think of it – what makes us collect anything? Is there a hoarding instinct in some of us, or all of us? A squirrel hoards nuts for the lean months whilst at times of national stress we've all seen supermarket shelves emptied quickly, but stamps? Or playing cards? I have collected various genres of transport models for decades, buses, trains and aircraft in big numbers, but why? There are private collectors of works of art; the value of their collections is not necessarily monetary but just as likely emotional, and probably not with an eye on an investment. Others will see collecting as a way of reliving their childhood, or an aspect of their life most dear to them.

Parents and grandparents will be familiar with children's obsession with collecting cards, maybe of footballers and here we see the

excitement of the chase, to obtain the vital last or rarest one to show off to their school friends and perhaps here we will find the psychology of collecting stamps; the pride in building up a collection, the hunt for the rarity or an 'error', a specialisation in itself that can vary enormously from a spelling mistake (embarrassing but not unknown) to missing colours or type.

Like collector-cards we saved in our youth, stamp collecting may well start with the fascination of issues from across the globe or from previous eras. A kindly aunt's birthday or Christmas present may see our first album with pages for a great many of the world's nations, and possibly an envelope of mixed stamps,

sometimes unused – mint – or maybe used and still on a fragment of the envelope. In this photograph of 'The Nelson' album we see just such an item, un-dated but this teenage owner (my wife) has made notes on the contents dated 1953-5. The hunt has begun, to piece together the perceived history of that collection as we are led by the album with the stamps scattered in all probability all over the dining-room table or the lounge carpet and before long the craving has developed, to add to this collection and then to multiply the number of albums needed to accommodate the growing collection until eventually order will need to be established. At that time, the likelihood is that there will be some sort

of concentration or specialisation, perhaps on specific countries or regions, or themes such as the subject of this series of books.

A great many stamp collectors concentrate on the country of their birth or home and build-up a comprehensive history of that nation's stamps into a portfolio of immense prestige that may even include text to provide a commentary or catalogue number. Another speciality is the study of the perforations that surround each stamp for ease of separating from the sheets, their size and hence the number on each edge, and to damage these devalues the stamp as much as a rip or thinning of the paper itself due to careless removal from its backing or the previously mentioned hinges. As postal authorities modernised and became more mechanised, stamps had watermarks added or phosphor strips which bore vital information. And then there is the collector with an eye on the investment for undoubtedly a great many stamps reward the serious collector very well and there are organisations that offer advice for the committed investor. Reading one of the established magazines on our subject will enlighten some and surprise others.

LOOKING AFTER STAMPS

That such a big industry, or some would say profession, has grown out of the love of a little piece of paper with gum on the back might be hard to credit but the obsession with the minutiae of the subject can sometimes seem out of all proportion.

Our Aunt's birthday present gave the young and budding philatelist the encouragement to either glue those precious stamps within the dotted squares provided or with wisdom find the little clear hinges that preserved them at least temporarily in place but today both these habits are discredited as they affect the stamp itself, for today the serious collector goes to incredible lengths to preserve each individual stamp in as near as possible the condition it left the printer. First of all, one should never touch the stamp itself; grease and other contaminants will over time degrade the surface whilst clumsy figures can quite easily crease or tear the delicate paper and perforations, so acquisition of specialised tweezers are a good idea, then take the trouble to look at the various types of album available.

Most will be ring-binders ready to accept the many different pages available. Some of these pages will have clear strips of varying depths to keep stamps secure and visible whilst others are available pre-printed with details of the country of origin and the specific issue to which it refers and it only remains for the owner to place his treasured morsel of paper behind special clear envelopes cut to size and ready for attaching to the designated space. Many will produce his or her own leaves, suitably annotated and presumably preserved in beautiful albums bound in leather. Many collectors exhibit their work at well-known exhibitions in city venues across the globe and their work is often lauded amongst their peers.

Finally, the collector must remember the bible of the stamp world – the catalogue. Here one will find a huge coming-together of stamps one wouldn't otherwise dream of, listed in copious detail by country and date to give a firm basis to any collection. Usually a value will also be provided, although one has to treat these with a little caution, as this is totally dependent on condition and the vagaries of market forces. Dependent upon the detail and how up-to-date one needs to be, these can be acquired for a few pounds or up to several hundreds for the most comprehensive, that from Stanley Gibbons stretching to several volumes at a cost running into the hundreds of pounds and whilst these are up-dated regularly, only the obsessive or professional will want to replace them regularly.

Having already been mentioned several times in this book and the series so far, I wish to acknowledge the work of Stanley Gibbons Ltd, stamp retailer and publisher of catalogues covering all countries as well as many specialised subjects, as well as the previously mentioned *Stamp Magazine*, without whose help this book would have been so much more difficult to produce.